D1196892

PLATONISM IN THE MIDWEST

PLATONISM IN THE MIDWEST

Paul R. Anderson

Temple University Publications
Distributed by Columbia University Press
New York and London 1963

To my wife, Ann,
who helped make this story possible

PREFACE

New interest has been shown, in recent years, in the process
by which American civilization has clarified its direction and
developed its own culture. This has resulted in study not
only of the highways but also of the byways of American
life, many of the latter having provided striking evidence of
the richness of the thought and life which have made America what it is. Increasingly, it is being recognized that no
one section of the country, no one hereditary strain, and no
one center of population has given definitive character to
our national life. The genius of America lies in the varied
impulses and sources which have given vitality to its existence.

To truly understand our heritage, therefore, we must do
more than merely hit the highlights of our political and economic history or picture our cultural development through
reference to a few great names. We must seek knowledge of
the less obvious forces and personalities which have left
their unheralded but indelible mark upon our past. George
Herbert Palmer once wisely remarked that "The tendencies
of an age appear more distinctly in its writers of inferior
rank than in those of commanding genius. These latter tell
of past and future as well as of the age in which they live.
They are for all time. But on the sensitive, responsive souls,

of less creative power, current ideals record themselves with clearness." [1] To give these lesser figures their due is oftentimes to cast significant light upon the age in which they lived.

This volume deals with a movement which has gone nearly unnoticed in American culture, yet which played a significant part in American life from 1860 to the 1890s. It was while working on another project with Professor Max H. Fisch that I discovered a few suggestive leads to the potential significance of the movement. Trips to important towns connected with this philosophical upsurge, and conferences with and letters from individuals who themselves had first-hand experiences to recount, furnished convincing evidence that here was a story worth telling before the materials necessary for its completion had passed out of existence. At first I thought that a brief monograph would provide adequate treatment of this intellectual facet of midwestern culture, but as sources multiplied and new evidence was uncovered nothing short of the scope of the present volume seemed sufficient for the task.

Dozens of people have given liberally of their time to make this story possible. To single out any for special mention would be to discriminate against others whose contributions have been of inestimable value. Suffice it to say that without the interest and kindness of many who have thought this epic worth recording no such detailed record could ever have emerged. Some of the materials in chapters two and four have already appeared in the *Journal of the Illinois State Historical Society,* and thanks are given to its editors

[1] George Herbert Palmer (ed.), *The English Works of George Herbert* (Boston, Houghton Mifflin, 1915), I, xii.

for permission to use them again here. Appreciation goes to Temple University Publications for its sponsorship.

If this story leaves the reader with a conviction as to the contributory importance of the byways in American culture it will have fulfilled one of its purposes. If it offers even partial enlightenment on the Midwest of the late nineteenth century it will have rewarded the author well.

CONTENTS

I.	The Midwest Comes of Age	1
II.	The Athens of the West	29
III.	The Metaphysical Giant	69
IV.	A Philosophic Outpost	119
V.	The Sage of the Osage	151
VI.	The Decline of Spirit	186
	Bibliography	203
	Index	209

PLATONISM IN THE MIDWEST

THE MIDWEST COMES OF AGE

"In the West people think more independently than in the East. The East is more learned, perhaps, but the West is doing more for civilization. In the West the people are more ready to learn what is said by diviner minds." The words were written by Bronson Alcott on his seventy-third birthday (November 29, 1872) which he spent in Dubuque, Iowa, on one of his frequent trips to the West. They were in no sense an attempt to humor the people of Dubuque but rather were the result of a studied judgment made after years of contact with the life and growing culture in the prairie country bordering the Mississippi River. To be sure, this judgment ran counter to that of his fellow New Englanders, who were accustomed to view their own section as the intellectual center of the country and who regarded everything west of the Hudson River (if not of the Connecticut) as little more than a market place for the land speculator or an unblazed trail for the pioneer. But Alcott was right. The West, or the Midwest as we more appropriately refer to it today, was intellectually, as well as agriculturally, fertile. This was particularly true in the realm of philosophy, for in the 1870s and 1880s the Mississippi Valley far surpassed the East in its productivity in this phase of culture and exerted considerable influence on the New England mind, as we shall see. The Midwest's philosophical supremacy was due largely to the influence of two movements, one centering around St. Louis and dominated by Hegel and the other centering around Jacksonville and Quincy, Illinois, and devoted to Plato. The second of these is the primary concern of this volume, but to grasp the significance of the growing maturity of the Midwest it is important to know something of both movements.

St. Louis was the gateway to the farther West by the middle of the nineteenth century, a thriving cosmopolitan city with a rapidly increasing population. It was here that the first philosophical movement took root. In 1857 William Torrey Harris (1835–1909), then twenty-two, moved to St. Louis to become a teacher of shorthand, soon changed to the public school system where he rose until he became superintendent of schools (1867), and later (1889), United States Commissioner of Education. The year after he arrived in St. Louis he met Henry C. Brokmeyer (1828–1906) who had come there by a circuitous route, after leaving Germany in his teens to escape military service. Brokmeyer was enthusiastic about Hegel, an enthusiasm which he had acquired from F. H. Hedge, a Unitarian minister in Providence while Brokmeyer was attending Brown and who had written *Prose Writers of Germany* (1848), in which he had included selections from Hegel. Brokmeyer interested Harris in Hegel and, being out of a job, he agreed to stay in St. Louis and translate Hegel's "Larger Logic" for Harris and two of his friends (George Stedman and J. H. Watters). This was the beginning of a movement which played an influential part in the intellectual life of America until the latter part of the century and even exerted influence early in this century. First was a discussion group, a Kant Club, so-called because its members were desirous of working back from Hegel, through his predecessors, to Kant. The Civil War prevented much increase in membership but by 1866 Brokmeyer had completed the translation, and Harris, who had continued his philosophical studies with increasing zest, was ready for larger undertakings. The result was the formation of the St. Louis Philosophical Society, with a much enlarged membership and a greater variety of interests and viewpoints. The next year the *Journal of Speculative Philosophy* (1867–93) came into existence, principally because there was considerable scholarly and literary ability in the group, but immediately because Harris had been rebuffed when he sent an article to Charles Eliot Norton for publication in the *North American Review*, and thereupon decided to edit a journal of his own. This came to be an important journal, both in America and abroad, for it was the first of its kind in the English language. In addition to its publication of first translations of a number of German philosophical writings, it was the natural organ for the expression of vigorous intellects who later came into philosophical prominence, men such as John Dewey, G. Stanley Hall, George H. Howison, William James, and Josiah Royce, in this country, and Edward Caird, J. H. Stirling, and W. Lutoslawski, abroad. Another journal was inspired by the St. Louis Movement, *The Western*, less important than the *Journal of Speculative Philosophy*, but exercising its own influence, particularly upon those interested in education and the arts; it lasted from 1872 until 1881.

The most important figures in the movement were Brokmeyer, Harris, Denton J. Snider (1841–1925), and Thomas Davidson (1840–1900). Brokmeyer was the inspiration of the movement and was the translator of Hegel's "Larger Logic" (which served as a sort of textbook), but was never philosophically articulate in his own right; he did produce two dramas, *The Errand Boy* and *A Foggy Night at Newport*, and a volume entitled *A Mechanic's Diary*. Harris was probably the outstanding mind in the group, rising in eminence to the extent that Nicholas Murray Butler could say of him (however much exaggerated), "I measure my words when I say that in my judgment Dr. Harris had the one truly great philosophical mind which has yet appeared on the western continent." [1] Harris was a great interpreter of the Hegelian system, a man of solid, clear thought who probably did more to promote philosophy, both in its theoretical and in its practical sense, than any man of his generation. Through his writings and lectures he provided interpretations of Hegelianism in religion, art, and education which affected the thinking of a wide public outside of those whose predominant interest was philosophy. Denton J. Snider was the most productive man in the group and probably the most original, although originality was no idol among these lovers of the classical and universal. During his lifetime he wrote upwards of fifty volumes, ranging from important studies of his "four bibles," Homer, Dante, Shakespeare, and Goethe, to philosophical treatises on the mind, the will, the state, and social institutions. Davidson was more or less the rebel of the group, the only really independent mind, but he was known more widely than anyone except Harris. He was an expert on the history of education and later was the organizer of a workers' college in New York and schools of philosophy at Farmington, Connecticut, and Glenmore, New York.

While the St. Louis Movement began with the reading of

---

[1] Charles M. Perry (ed.), *The St. Louis Movement in Philosophy: Some Source Material* (Norman, University of Oklahoma Press, 1930), p. 51.

Hegel, it was no mere society to glorify him. The German sage was simply the center of an orbit, the total contemplation of which encompassed every significant human enterprise. These people felt they were engaged in important undertakings, the meaning of which was to be found in the Hegelianism which united them. To be sure, the movement had its greatest effect in philosophy but it also exerted influence in education, art, and literature. Many of the members were in education, professionally, and their impact was widely felt. Six of them wrote significant treatises in the field, and the influence which Harris, as United States Commissioner of Education, had upon the normal schools and upon educational theory in general is unquestioned. Susan Blow, one of the prominent women members, was a pioneer in the kindergarten movement.

In art there was less interest in creation than in understanding. Harris often wrote on the subject, and the preface to the first volume of the *Journal of Speculative Philosophy* reminded its readers that about one third of the material included therein had to do with art. Davidson and Snider wrote significant volumes in the field, as did William H. Bryant, another member. It has already been remarked that Snider was an authority in literature, but he was only one of a large number who gave time to such figures as Dante and Shakespeare. Literary classes and schools were founded in St. Louis and elsewhere. J. K. Hosmer wrote a *Short History of German Literature*. Brokmeyer was joined by Snider and J. G. Woerner in the writing of plays, and Snider and Woerner each wrote novels.

Social problems were not neglected either. Woerner, J. C. Learned, A. E. Kroeger, and B. A. Hill, as well as Snider, wrote on political and economic subjects Woerner, a judge, was primarily interested in the philosophy of law; Learned and Hill devoted their time to economic theory and practice; Kroeger and Snider concentrated more on government.

This is no mean record for an organization whose members were amateurs, men and women who at best could give only a portion of their time to philosophical pursuits.[2] But it was paralleled by a comparable movement, the Platonic, with which this volume is particularly concerned. This movement had as its chief centers Jacksonville and Quincy, Illinois, and took as its ultimate inspiration and guide Plato rather than Hegel. Platonism took hold in the Midwest in 1860, two years after Hegelianism and under similar circumstances, with the formation of a small Plato Club which Dr. Hiram K. Jones (1818–1903) headed in Jacksonville. Since Jacksonville was not as large as St. Louis and there was much communication between Illinois towns, it was natural for a movement such as this to spread rapidly. Clubs were soon organized in Quincy, Decatur, and Bloomington, although Quincy was the only one of these towns where the movement achieved real prominence. After the Plato Club had been in existence for over twenty years, it inspired another organization, the American Akademe, which aimed at a cos-

---

[2] For a fuller account of the St. Louis movement, refer to Charles M. Perry (ed.), *The St. Louis Movement in Philosophy: Some Source Material* (Norman, University of Oklahoma Press, 1930); Edward L. Schaub (ed.), *William Torrey Harris, 1835–1935* (Chicago, The Open Court Publishing Co., 1936); Denton J. Snider, *The St. Louis Movement in Philosophy, Literature, Education, with Chapters of Autobiography* (St. Louis, Sigma Publishing Co., 1920); and D. H. Harris (ed.), *A Brief Report of the Meeting Commemorative of the Early St. Louis Movement* (Los Angeles, 1922). Were a complete picture of the development of culture in the Midwest to be attempted, much more attention would have to be given to the St. Louis Movement than is done here. Another Hegelian influence, quite independent of the St. Louis Movement, existed in Ohio: see Loyd D. Easton, "Hegelianism in Nineteenth Century Ohio," *Journal of the History of Ideas*, XXIII (1962) 355–78.

mopolitan membership, much larger than that of the St. Louis Philosophical Society. Three magazines came into existence, *The Platonist*, the *Bibliotheca Platonica* and the *Journal of the American Akademe*, all with international circulation, although none had quite the continuous influence or permanent importance of the *Journal of Speculative Philosophy*. The Platonic movement produced one outstanding thinker, Dr. Jones, and one exceptional scholar, Thomas M. Johnson (1851–1919). In these two, the movement had men who compared favorably with the leaders of the St. Louis Movement. Jones was classed with Harris as one of the two outstanding attractions at the Concord School of Philosophy (1879–88) and Johnson's translations were comparable to those produced by the members of the St. Louis Movement.[3]

The Platonic and Hegelian movements were more than phases of provincial culture; they were intellectual forces with national and international influence and had to be reckoned with by the larger public. The form in which they came to be expressed, adult group education, was soon to be adopted elsewhere under their aegis. Philosophical societies and summer schools sprang up all the way from Chicago to Concord, Massachusetts. To speak briefly of the most important of these will give some idea of the vitality of this midwestern development.

The Chicago Philosophical Society was formed in 1873 around a nucleus supplied by a group which General N. B. Buford had established several years earlier. The motive of the society was defined in the constitution as "the mutual improvement of its members and the general diffusion of knowledge." The subjects to be included were moral philos-

[3] Details will be reserved for later chapters.

ophy, social science, natural science, speculative philosophy, and current history. When the organization actually got under way the great preponderance of topics discussed had to do with the first and fourth subjects. The creation of this society was due in large part to the example of its predecessors in St. Louis and central Illinois. Samuel Willard, one of the prominent members of the Plato Club in Jacksonville, was one of the charter members of the Chicago organization, having moved to Chicago; Willard gave more addresses before the organization than any other single figure. Harris and Davidson were made honorary members and they and Snider spoke before the group. So did Hiram K. Jones, Charles Caverno, and Louis Block of the Jacksonville society. Take away the influence of the Hegelian and Platonic schools, and the Chicago organization would have been bereft of its core. Its greatest period of activity was in the late 1870s; it died out in the late 1880s, having in the interim been superseded by the Concord School and the American Akademe and having succumbed to the same influences which later sounded the death knell for all of these organizations.

Under the influence of the Platonic movement, Dr. James E. Garretson delivered weekly lectures in the Hospital of Oral Surgery in Philadelphia, during the early 1880s. He tried to secure an endowment for a permanent school of philosophy but his efforts failed. An American Institute of Christian Philosophy was organized in 1881 and held summer meetings at Greenwood Lake, New York, but this too was not of long duration.

The Concord School of Philosophy was the most significant of the various attempts at philosophical education for adults. Its origin went back to 1840, when Emerson and Alcott had hopes of establishing a permanent institution

for philosophical lectures and discussion but found no possibility for its realization at the time. Alcott never lost
sight of this hope and on his various trips west kept sowing
seeds for its ultimate fruition. In the early 1870s Mrs.
Sarah Denman of Quincy offered to buy the Wayside Inn in Concord for this purpose but financial pressure later forced her
to withdraw the offer. The school finally got under way in
1879 after a two-week trial session during the previous summer, at which Hiram K. Jones was the center of attraction.
Alcott had long been anxious to have some of the midwest-
erners go east to mix with the Concord people. On this occasion (1878) Dr. and Mrs. Jones and Mrs. Elizur Wolcott
and her daughters from Jacksonville and Mrs. Denman and
Mrs. Ebenezer Baldwin from Quincy were guests. Harris
had been invited too but he was unable to go. This left the
stage clear for Dr. Jones, who captivated the guests in their
nightly assemblages in the homes of Alcott, Emerson, and
J. H. Sanborn. On July 14, Alcott wrote: "I question
whether one chair of philosophy in any of our colleges can
deal as ably with pure metaphysics as our friend from the
prairies of Illinois. We here in New England have listened
to nothing concerning Plato comparable to his interpretations and statements of that supreme idealist." The following day he wrote: "We were mostly questioners and listeners
during the evening's discussion, being most of us assured
that a master had come amongst us to whom it was not only
a delight but a culture to listen with reverence and docil-
ity." [4] When the visit was over Alcott held that the name of
Hiram K. Jones should be included in any list of outstanding
Concord figures for he had brought additional renown to the
town. Sanborn, who was something of a journalist as well
as an educator, wrote concerning Jones: "He has carried

[4] MS, Diary for 1878.

much farther than Mr. Emerson that minute and patient study of Plato which is necessary to comprehend him; and, though he lacks the rapid sure insight of our Concord scholar, he makes up for it by a method as positive and searching as that of the old philosophers." [5]

The West had brought philosophy back to the East with new power. Yet this was only the beginning of an organization which was to be largely dominated, at least in its early years, by the figures from the Midwest. Before the Illinois visitors had left Concord they had agreed to return the following summer and take part in the projected Concord School of Philosophy. When it opened on July 12, 1879, the chief lecturers were Harris and Jones. S. H. Emery, of Quincy, who had rented the Orchard House from Alcott, was made director of the school and a large proportion of those who attended were people from the Midwest. This was an eye-opener for complacent New Englanders. Louisa May Alcott thoroughly enjoyed the shock which came to the natives. She said:

People laugh, but will enjoy something new in this dull old town; and the fresh Westerners will show them that all the culture of the world is not in Concord. I had a private laugh when Mrs. _____ asked one of the newcomers, with her superior air, if she had ever looked into Plato. And the modest lady from Jacksonville answered, with a twinkle at me, "We have been reading Plato in Greek for the past six years." Mrs. _____ subsided after that.[6]

Harris and Jones were clearly the outstanding lecturers, respectively presenting the claims of Hegel and Plato. This led to a natural competition, and the listeners divided into

---

[5] *Springfield Republican,* July 26, 1878.
[6] E. D. Cheney, *Louisa May Alcott* (Boston, Roberts, 1889) p. 320.

rival camps under the two leaders. Snider stated this rather succinctly when he said:

The two main threads of the school were now spun alongside of each other by those two ardent philosophic spinners, Dr. Harris and Dr. Jones, propagandists of Hegel and Plato respectively. Between these two speakers, as well as between their doctrines, there was felt to be a gently throbbing undercurrent of rivalry, amicable but still somewhat frictional, which made perceptibly warmer the interest in the cold abstractions of metaphysics. Each leader had his followers in the audience, and both sides kept watching intently the tournament, yet with impartial sympathy determined to give the palm to the best man.[7]

This rivalry continued for four years when the victory went to Harris and Hegel, partly because of their increasing support and partly because of default. In the second year of the school, Mrs. Elizabeth Thompson of New York gave $1,000 for the construction of Hillside Chapel where the meetings were held from that time on; the structure still exists in Concord. The school was more than a battlefield for the defenders of Hegel and Plato; it became a mecca for everyone interested in philosophy. Its themes were varied and its lecturers were well-known.

The Concord School attempted to serve the same needs which brought the midwestern groups into prominence. Despite rivalry, the driving zeal of those most intimately associated with the school was to rise above the growing materialism of the day and view life in some coherent pattern. James McCosh of Princeton expressed the underlying unity of purpose as follows:

Those who met were drawn together by a common faith and sentiment not easily defined (the school is not much inclined to

---

[7] *The St. Louis Movement in Philosophy, Literature, Education with Chapters of Autobiography* (St. Louis, Sigma, 1920), pp. 307–8.

lay restraints on itself by definition), yet noticeable by all. They constitute a school quite as much as the ancient Pythagoreans, the Platonists, and Neoplatonists, with whom they have certain interesting affinities. They believe in mind as infinitely higher than matter,—some of them believe in matter simply as a veil thrown over mind. They are sure that in mind there is vastly more than sense, than sight or touch or hearing. Some of them would burst the bounds of space and time, which so hem them in, and go out into the eternal, the infinite, the absolute. They are seeking to mount to a sphere far above the mundane, and if they do not rise to the sky, which is apt to become ever more remote as we ascend, they at least, as in a balloon, reach the clouds whence, as the traveller in the Alps, they gain grand views of the heavens above them and lovely views of the green vales below them.[8]

The Concord School closed in 1888 but it had two successors, both of which were led by Thomas Davidson, product of midwestern philosophy. During the last years of the Concord School and as a prelude to its meetings Davidson had assembled his followers at St. Cloud, New Jersey, for a few days' seasoning. The year in which the Concord School closed he set up his own school at Farmington, Conn., meetings being scheduled for a two weeks' period. The school lasted for three years. The courses for 1890 were representative. In that year topics included the philosophy of T. H. Green, the relations of church and state, the Greek moralists, and the primary concepts of economic science. Davidson taught the course on the Greek moralists, while lectures in the other courses were delivered by such men as H. N. Gardiner of Smith College, John Dewey, and Harris. In the summer of 1890, Davidson and some of his close friends spent a short time at Glenmore, near Keene, New York, in the Adirondacks, and found the spot so delightful that the

[8] "The Concord School of Philosophy," *Princeton Review*, n.s. 9 (1881), 49–50.

following year Farmington was abandoned and a school in Glenmore set up to take its place. With the change in location a more pretentious plan was introduced, the school operating from July to October inclusive, divided into two periods of two months each. It continued until the late 1890s and offered a program in philosophy and the other humanities of greater breadth than any of its predecessors. The school never had the wide public appeal of Concord, but it did bring together for consultation and discussion a great many of the coming scholars of the period.[9]

From St. Louis and central Illinois, therefore, philosophy traveled back to New England and provided its culture with a new leaven. The vigor in propagation which gave the Platonic and Hegelian movements such widespread influence was rooted in depth of thought and strength of purpose. These qualities were quickly apparent to a man like Alcott, for example, whose conviction as to the superiority of the western mind was based upon personal observation.

Alcott first came into contact with philosophical activity in the Midwest when he spent several weeks in St. Louis on his 1858–59 lecture tour. He was in daily association with the Harris-Brokmeyer group and soon found himself over his head in abstract analysis. When he returned to Concord he and Emerson acquired simplified accounts of Hegel but these were of no great help. The Civil War prevented Alcott's return to St. Louis until 1866, when he spent four weeks in another attempt to make something of the Hegelian conversations to which he listened. When he returned again in 1870 he still couldn't "follow them intelligently." By this

[9] For further information concerning Davidson's schools, refer to William Knight, (ed.), *Memorials of Thomas Davidson* (Boston, Ginn, 1907), chaps. X and XI.

time the *Journal of Speculative Philosophy* was publishing its fifth volume. Alcott wrote about this journal:

Nothing seemed less likely four years ago than that a magazine would appear on the western side of the Mississippi devoted to the profoundest speculation and displaying in the writers an equality, both by scholarship and acumen, to the subjects undertaken, or if any seemed less likely, it was that if such a publication did appear [it] should live beyond a second number. Yet here it is successfully entering upon its fifth volume. And the wonder is the greater since it has made no compromise with the popular intelligence, none with the popular radicalism, none with the popular conservatism, none with that desire for copy reading to which our American scholars have largely succumbed.[10]

The more Alcott traveled the more he became convinced of the vitality of the western mind. In Dubuque, Iowa, he discovered Mrs. Austin Adams, the sibylline oracle, with whom he carried on a lengthy correspondence for years. In Jacksonville, he met with Dr. Jones' Plato Club and expressed considerable surprise at finding students of Plato and Neoplatonism reading in the original Greek and engaging in discussions of high calibre on Platonic themes. In Quincy he was deeply impressed by Mrs. Sarah Denman and Samuel H. Emery, Jr. and the philosophical discussions which they inspired. In Bloomington, Illinois, in Davenport, Iowa, and elsewhere he met educated and thoughtful groups unparalleled by anything he knew in New England. After such a trip he could earnestly write: "A six month's appearance here in these western cities might dissipate many prejudices prevailing at the East concerning the culture and accomplishments of the people in these parts."[11] So impressed was he by the intellectual climate of the area that

---

[10] MS, "Western Evenings: An Itinerary," 1870–71, p. 58.
[11] *Ibid.*, p. 239.

he said he was cautioned by his friends at home not to "forget my loyalty to eastern queens and lose my heart on the ladies of Dubuque and the West." [12] Alcott's journals were sprinkled liberally with praise for these western people. No one had a better right to speak than Alcott for he literally spent weeks in these western towns, absorbing something of the spirit as well as the content of the discussions at the same time that he provided outside stimulation. Alcott's judgment was no fiction of the imagination nor was it an exaggeration of the facts. The Midwest did have its culture and its philosophy as many another New Englander discovered for himself when, through the Concord School and otherwise, these prairie philosophers exerted a regenerative influence on their own languid intellectual life.

The Mississippi valley was neither lacking in culture nor merely copying from New England. It supported two independent, thriving philosophical movements, both finding common cause in the need they served, both nourishing the minds of nearly two generations of people at home, and both finding a wider public elsewhere, eager and anxious for the message they bore. This development was no commonplace of American history. Neither was it a result of geographic chance. It was a result of converging forces at work in the life of the area. Knowledge of these forces will not only explain the origin of the philosophical movements but it will also make their existence seem natural, if not necessary.

Alcott must have cherished an inner sense of joy when he realized that the influence of New England was at least one factor in making philosophy possible in the Midwest, particularly since he and Emerson were such important instru-

---

[12] *Ibid.,* p. 120. The reference to "the ladies" was due to the fact that they constituted a large proportion of the membership of the clubs he visited although the leaders were usually men.

mentalities. The background of many of the leading figures, particularly in the Platonic movement, was that of New England. Mrs. Denman and Emery, in Quincy, were both born and raised in New England, as were many others. A goodly number had gone east to school. In Jacksonville, the "Yale Band," which founded Illinois College, and the instructors who were brought from the East had their proportionate influence.

New England background alone, however, was a minor factor. More important was the predominance of New England writers. When the people of the Midwest turned to reading, one of their main sources was eastern literature. Emerson was particularly influential because his writings had become American classics. Dr. Jones got his first philosophical thrill when he read Emerson, Thomas M. Johnson read him early, and most of the others in Jacksonville and Quincy had also read the Concord sage. But personal factors were also involved. Harris, in St. Louis, secured his first philosophical interest from Alcott when Alcott lectured at Yale in 1857, and Brokmeyer became interested in Hegel, as has been said before, through Hedge, in Providence. Not only was the initial impulse given in part by New England transcendentalism but continued stimulation was also provided by Emerson and Alcott on their numerous trips west. It should not be inferred, however, that these movements were largely an offshoot of New England culture. Indigenous forces were even more important than New England contacts.

First among these was increased leisure time, which led to a desire for self-improvement. By the second half of the century the area concerned was no longer a real frontier, however the Back Bay mind might regard it. It was settling

down to a more composed existence while the petty entre-
preneurs and adventurous land pirates were moving much
further west. All of the cities concerned were prosperous,
even if not wealthy. This fact provided an untouched reser-
voir of energy and interest which would have been impossible
under more primitive living conditions. These people combined vitality and a desire for self-development so that leisure time became an opportunity for culture and an increase
of learning.

The basic equalitarianism of midwest life provided a lively
sense of democratic values in education and culture. Education was increasingly regarded, not as a veneer for those of
means, but rather a necessity for everyone. The arts were in
like manner regarded not as an exclusive possession of a
class, but as a desirable source of enrichment for people on
all economic levels. As solutions for basic economic problems
were found it was natural for those without education,
formal or otherwise, to seek it and for those with education,
however limited or extensive, to want more. Having at least
partially solved the problem of making a living these people
gave increasing attention to finding reason and joy in living.
The fruits of culture were spread widely. Periodicals serving
varied needs appeared in abundance. Discussion groups and
study clubs, many of which became national organizations,
were organized on a large scale. The country editor played
an important part, too, for he was a leader of thought in
the community. It is no mere figure of speech to say that
farm boys followed the plow with book in hand, be it Shakespeare, Emerson, or Thoreau. There was less illiteracy in
this section of the country than anywhere else. Combined
with a democratic love of knowledge was an absence of what
Channing referred to as "the yoke of opinion," that subtle

restraining force which prevents the free development of the individual and stunts the courage necessary for creative thought and action. Prejudice and convention existed in the Midwest as well as elsewhere, but these had not yet shackled the minds of the growing generation.

The Midwest began to achieve maturity in culture just when New England was courting complacency. One author says of New England:

In the mild air of the early eighties, a haze of Indian summer hung over New England. The heats and the rigors of the past were long forgotten, the passions of the war, the old crusades, and a mood of reminiscence possessed the people, for whom the present offered few excitements. Society had lost its vital interests, and the Boston mind was indolent and flaccid, as if the struggle for existence had passed it by. Its ambition seemed to be atrophied, except on the practical plane, and this was equally true in the rural regions. Many a clock had gone dead in hamlets that had hummed with life, where the men, it was often remarked, were torpid and listless; and farmers sat in the village stores, wagging their beards all day, chewing and whittling, as shiftless Canadian thistles. The old strain was wearing out, or so the Boston people said; but the region was tranquil and mellow, at least on the surface.[13]

This vivid characterization may exaggerate the condition of New England society, but it does suggest a degree of lethargy neither characteristic of nor acceptable in the Midwest. The Midwest was neither coasting on the momentum of the past nor tired of activity itself. Its spirit was that of youth, enthusiastic, courageous, and self-confident. Its driving zeal for improvement was the psychological urge which brought on maturity. As a result, the Midwest came of age, and the

[13] Van Wyck Brooks, *New England: Indian Summer, 1865–1915* (New York, E. P. Dutton, 1940), p. 330.

philosophical development with which we are concerned here was an important part of this process.

The equalitarian attitude toward education and culture tended to break down not only barriers between classes but also barriers between the sexes. It was no mere accident that the feminist movement had greater strength in the Midwest than elsewhere, that Sorosis of Jacksonville and Friends in Council of Quincy were two of the earliest women's clubs in the country, that the first coeducational institution in the country was in Ohio (Oberlin), that Mississippi was the first state to grant women control over their own property, that Kansas first permitted them to vote in school elections, and that Wyoming was the first state to grant complete equality in the franchise. The breakdown of the doctrine of sex inequality was an important factor in strengthening the philosophical movements at St. Louis and in Illinois. Many women in the St. Louis group held prominent positions in the city school system. In the Jacksonville and Quincy groups there were more women than men and all of the leading ones were outspoken believers in women's rights. Women were desirous of demonstrating their equality in all lines and to turn to philosophy, generally regarded as one of the most difficult of disciplines, was to add weight to their cause. Without the backing which women gave to these movements, their vitality and influence would have been decidedly weakened.

The Hegelian and Platonic movements began at the time of the Civil War when social problems were important and when these problems stood out because the cities involved were all near the borderline of the South. Bitter strife existed between the protagonists of freedom and the supporters of state rights. The issues of individual versus state, state versus nation, race versus race, and nation versus nation were paramount. These issues, with the possible exception of the last, were not abstract ones, but touched everyday activities. Hiram K. Jones, for example, had an underground tunnel running into his own home, where he is said to have kept runaway slaves, for he, as well as most of his friends, was opposed to slavery; threats and intimidations because of such action and its verbal defense were not uncommon. Such intimate contact with seething issues might well have led to concentration on social welfare. Instead it led to a desire for an inclusive philosophy which would offer an interpretation of experience in universal terms. These people sought to rise above conflicts and view them as episodes in the unfolding of an all-embracing plan. They were not exponents of social programs; they were interpreters of social events on a cosmic scale. Some attention was given to social philosophy in St. Louis, and Hiram Jones gave speeches on topics of a social nature ranging from "Heredity in Crime" to "Asiatic Cholera—Its History, Causes, Prevention and Cure," but these interests were derivative from philosophic positions which were universal in scope. A quotation from Jones will serve to explain this.

Certain important matters especially embracing human rights and interests are never settled until they get settled a-right; no number of votes can make wrong right; and secondly ideas and first principles rule ultimately. They are never merely passive elements. Their fruits mature in blessing or retribution even after men have repudiated them.[14]

Jones believed that no moral expedient offers a solution to a problem, that only as one has knowledge of first principles can he understand the ups and downs of social policy and action. This attitude, characteristic of these midwestern fig-

[14] MS, "The Phillipino War," 1900.

ures, was not a defense of inaction but rather expressive of a belief in a universal law of morality which ultimately rules. Moral problems, therefore, were not autonomous; their solutions were to be based on religious and metaphysical principles. It was to these principles that they gave attention rather than to active participation in ameliorative measures.

They regarded self-education as the key to the solution of ethical issues. After the Civil War, as is common to all postwar periods, the dislocation of normal patterns of living led to a wave of crime and licentiousness. Cities like Springfield, Illinois (not far from Jacksonville), where large military establishments existed, were infested with prostitutes and were the scene of many a bloody brawl. Persons and property were freely attacked. At one time, for example, General John Cook felt compelled to order two companies to serve as moral guardians in Springfield. This wave of crime inspired the organization of many reform societies; a revived temperance movement, among these, gathered momentum. But it was not the practice of the philosophically-minded people of St. Louis, Jacksonville, and Quincy, to give more than generous sympathy to these. Instead, regarding education as the panacea, they sought to develop a philosophy which provided knowledge of moral truth—assuming, in true Socratic manner, that if men knew the truth they would act in accordance with it.

Serious interest in Hegel and Plato was partly the result of a desire for philosophic knowledge which would provide a gospel of social unity. After the war there was a strong current of nationalism, nowhere more present than in the Midwest. There was a desire not only for the unity of North and South, but also for the unity of East and West. Hegelianism provided a gospel for the occasion on one pattern, based on logical synthesis of opposing forces. Platonism provided it on another pattern, based not on rigid logic but rather on belief in the fundamental harmony of reality: unity was not the result of synthesizing opposites, but was pure originally; conflict could be eliminated, therefore, the closer man approached knowledge of original perfection. Both schools served the same need in terms of providing a philosophy *of* union and a philosophy *for* union. The demand, commonly expressed at the time, for an American philosophy was a part of the current nationalism. The philosophically-minded people in the Midwest were conscious of this demand and tried to fill it. Harris said what was needed was not American thought but American thinkers. What he meant by this was that the need was not for something new in thinking which distinguished American thought from the thought of other national groups, but rather for some clear thinkers who could understand and interpret the universal in philosophy, best expressed (from Harris' point of view) in Hegel and to a lesser degree in Plato. Jones conceived of the American Akademe as an organ through which this same kind of recreative thought could be achieved. The difficulty in the thinking of both the Hegelian and Platonic schools was in assuming that a philosophy provided for America was the same thing as, or better than, a philosophy developed in America. But that both schools thought a return to classical fountains of truth would provide a unifying philosophy in this country is unquestioned, however unsuccessful the final results.

Important also for understanding the genesis of these philosophical groups were certain religious tendencies at the time. The first of these was a vigorous revivalism after the close of the war. Big mass conversions took place in all the larger cities and considerable gains were made in the membership of all denominations; this was largely the result of an emotional reaction and was totally displeasing to the more intellectual segment of society, at least as represented by the philosophical groups. Coupled with this emotional outburst in religion was a considerable amount of internal strife, particularly in the Presbyterian and Episcopal folds, caused by feuds over the issue of slavery and disagreement over liturgical and institutional matters; these inner conflicts again left the more moderate elements cold. The "moderates" distrusted institutionalized forms and rigid indoctrination, and they organized a great many independent religious societies, a development which Alcott encouraged and praised. The Hegelian and Platonic movements served to bring together a great many such essentially religious, yet independent, minds. The tendency in philosophical circles was not to deny Christianity but to view Christianity as one religion among many, all of them representative in varying degrees of true religion. The Transcendentalist movement had served the same function in New England a generation earlier.

While midwestern philosophy was opposed to the prevailing conservatism in religion it tended to align itself on the side of religion when a common enemy came into view. To see how this happened it is necessary to understand another force which, by reaction, tended to throw the liberal and conservative religionists together. This force was the materialistic tendency of the period, in action and in thought.

The growing prosperity of the country in the last half of the century made education and culture possible, as has been pointed out, but it also led to a life of luxury. The Gilded Age, as the period has been called, was accompanied by lavish concern for the accoutrements of life. The height of this development has been characterized in the following manner:

In lavish expenditures as well as in exotic performances, pleasures were hungrily sought by the fretful rich delivered from the bondage of labor and responsibility. Diamonds were set in teeth; a private carriage and personal valet were provided for a pet monkey; dogs were tied with ribbons to the back seats of Victorias and driven out in the park for airings; a necklace costing $600,000 was purchased for a daughter of Croesus; $65,000 was spent for a dressing table, $75,000 for a pair of opera glasses. An entire theatrical company was taken from New York to Chicago to entertain the friends of a magnate and a complete orchestra engaged to serenade a new-born child. In a burst of sentimental benevolence a family of destitute Negroes in the South was suddenly dowered with riches, garbed in luxury, and placed in a gorgeous house.[15]

Obviously this was not equally true throughout the Midwest, particularly in the smaller towns, but what was true of the large cities such as Chicago was true of the smaller places in proportion. Whereas the building of luxurious town houses and the establishment of private art collections was characteristic of the big cities, less ambitious but nevertheless pretentious Victorian residences and comparable gluttony were found elsewhere. The things of life multiplied rapidly and a love of their possession was general and widespread. Possession became an end in itself and the expenditure of time and money on the trivial and frivolous became a competitive sport. This tendency in the end was to play a prominent part in the demise of the development now under consideration, but not without a battle. Still unemancipated

[15] Charles and Mary Beard, *The Rise of American Civilization* (New York, Macmillan, 1927), II, 392.

from the thrift and simplicity which their religious ancestry had grafted upon them, many of the people in the Midwest recoiled from the growing preoccupation with the mundane. They longed for knowledge of something more permanent than the mere vogue of the moment. They sought understanding and this was not to be found in things. They wanted a source of internal security and this was not provided by absorption in the procurement of goods. So they turned to philosophy and found there a tradition which met their elemental needs, which gave them reason for living, discipline for daily action, and hope for the future.

Ethical materialism was revolting but so was metaphysical materialism. The latter was much strengthened by the theory of organic evolution, which by the seventies was well known in the United States. Darwin's *Origin of Species* came out in 1859 but the impact of the theory was hardly felt for a decade, after which it dealt increasingly crushing blows to the traditional theory of origins and in turn to the concept of man as a spiritual being. Darwin's theory did not create this intellectual revolution alone. Herbert Spencer's philosophy, which applied the evolutionary idea to all fields of human endeavor, gave evolutionism popularity and set its implications in clear perspective. Spencer quickly came to be the vogue in America. He was given money by Americans to aid him in prosecuting his studies and the sale of his books was much greater here than in England. Spencer conceived of man as the product of an orderly process in nature rather than as the direct creation of God. Man's interests were those of adjustment to the world in which he lived, not emancipation from it. Human institutions were products of the changing conditions of existence, neither to be traced to basic forms nor to be assumed to be permanent.

Life was a process of development in which man sought more effective adjustment, the forms of which were relative to circumstances of time and place. Without going into detail it can readily be seen that a philosophy of this sort was revolutionary, at least as viewed by those for whom religion was important and by those whose religious beliefs were traditionally rooted. Clash between evolutionary thought and traditional religion was inevitable. For the traditionalist, there was a stable frame of reference for nature and for institutions; man was a divine creation; his soul was separable and immortal; his life was an episode in the career of this immortal essence; his activities were to be evaluated in terms of how closely they approximated the pattern of the divine. Not one of these beliefs stood unchallenged by the evolutionary mode of thinking. The result was strife. Some men went all the way with Spencer and read out of the picture most customary belief. Others, strong believers in traditional religion, shrank even from consideration of the validity of the new doctrines and became more deeply ingrained in their own conservatism. An even greater number stood in between, torn by conflicting attitudes and beliefs and desirous of reconciling the old and the new. In the main the midwestern philosophers fell into this third group. They were not hidebound but neither were they completely openminded. They did not want to renounce the new *in toto* but neither would they accept it wholeheartedly. They were looking for something permanent behind the changing panorama of experience since the temporary and passing failed to provide sufficient moral and intellectual satisfaction. They thought of man as something more than a mere biological phenomenon, for his material accomplishments alone were taken as evidence of a higher origin and a higher destiny.

They were never enthusiastic, therefore, over the new gospel of evolution (which seemed to end in materialism). Anxious to preserve the essentials of the old (which they regarded not as true because they were old, but old because they were true), they opposed much of the new. This placed them, in effect, on the side of the traditionalists, for they strongly defended the permanent as opposed to the changing, the certain as opposed to the probable, and the absolute as opposed to the relative.

The midwestern philosophers read Spencer even if they could not accept his point of view. Harris, for example, wrote a long critical summary of Spencer's philosophy in the first issue of the *Journal of Speculative Philosophy*. He commended Spencer by saying that thought like his was at least an indication of philosophical activity. He pointed out, however, that the difficulty with thinking of this sort was that it failed to reach the highest stage in the knowing process, that which he called "comprehension"; it was limited to the world of phenomena in its judgments and yet was actually predicated on categories higher than experience; because of this it was insufficient and inadequate. In the Jacksonville group, there was no disinclination to deal with Spencer, but every attempt was made to show his deficiencies. The attack which these people made upon Spencer and the new evolutionary point of view was not, to be sure, that of categorical denial (as was most often the case with the traditionalists) but rather one based upon analysis. The technique of criticism on the part of traditional religion and the philosophically minded was different, but the total effect of their effort to discredit Spencer was much the same. It will be seen later that the growing influence of the evolutionary view was one of the causes for the decline of philosophy in the Midwest, but it is sufficient here to point out that the challenge which Spencer and others made to religion gave power to these movements, in part as defense for traditional religion and in part as acceptable substitutes for it.

In summary, then, the culture of the Midwest was fertile during and after the Civil War, philosophical study was an important phase of the growing maturity of this section of the country, and this development extended its influence far and wide. Philosophical activity was a natural outgrowth of the convergence of economic, social and religious, as well as personal, factors at work during the period. With this orientation we shall take leave of the Hegelian movement except in a minor way and concentrate on the origin and growth of Platonism as one important expression of the temper of the age.

CHAPTER II

THE ATHENS OF THE WEST

Recognition that men and movements are not born in vacuums and that their fulfillment is possible only in terms of temporal and social considerations is now a commonplace among historians of thought. A productive soil is considered to be just as necessary for the full development of ideas as it is for botanical species. This social soil, however, is of two distinct types, one consisting of the broad underlying tendencies of a period and the other of the local causes which bring a given tendency to the fore. Up to this point we have seen some of the deeper forces which gave the Hegelian and Platonic schools reason for being. As we turn now to the Platonic movement in particular, it is important to understand the local factors which made Jacksonville, rather than Springfield or other cities, the center of Platonism. In this regard it is not enough merely to know that Jacksonville was an early town or that it was on the first railroad in Illinois or that it was the place where Stephen A. Douglas learned his law and where William Jennings Bryan secured his education. Only as one realizes that the whole character of Jacksonville was such as to inspire interest in culture does it seem natural for philosophy to spring from its soil.

From its very inception Jacksonville was marked as a city

of institutions. Even two years before the town was laid out (1825), the Morganian Society had been organized to prevent the introduction of slavery into the state. From that day until the present, it has been a center of clubs, organizations, philanthropic societies, welfare and educational institutions. Earliest among the clubs was Sigma Pi, founded in 1843 on the Illinois College campus during the period when the college fraternity movement had its greatest expansion, and followed soon by Phi Alpha (1845). Other men's clubs, such as the Literary Union, The Club, and the Round Table later became established in city life. In addition to the Antislavery Society, others such as the Natural History Society, the Historical Society, the Microscopic Society, and even an Anti-Horse-Stealing Society, were added. Women's societies, too, played an early part in Jacksonville life. The first of these was The Ladies Association for Educating Females (later changed to the Ladies Education Society), a philanthropic society founded in 1832 for the purpose of providing scholarships and giving other necessary aid to women seeking an education. This particular organization led to the establishment of others of its kind in New York City, Rochester, Chicago, Springfield, Illinois, and elsewhere. Sorosis, the first women's literary organization in the country, was established locally in 1868, shortly after the first group was organized in New York. State institutions for the blind, deaf, and insane were all founded in Jacksonville during the 1840s, and for nearly ten years the asylum for feeble-minded children was also located there; these state institutions brought with them as administrators and instructors a number of people who made significant contributions to the cultural life of the community.

In the realm of secondary and collegiate education the city was also abundantly supplied. Illinois College accepted its first students in 1830, although its charter was not granted until 1835; it was one of the earliest colleges in the state. The Jacksonville Female Academy was chartered in the same year and continued independently until its amalgamation with Illinois College in 1903. Illinois Female College (now MacMurray College) was founded in 1846 and received its full college charter in 1863. A third college was established in 1856 (Berean College), but this was discontinued in 1859. In 1846 the Young Ladies' Athenaeum was established with a course of instruction based largely on the Pestalozzian system, a radical departure in educational procedure at the time; this school was discontinued near the close of the century. In addition to these was the Jacksonville Business College (founded in 1865) which, for a period of years, offered a limited number of liberal arts, as well as vocational, courses. Two flourishing conservatories of music vied for public support in the last quarter of the century. For several years (1843–48) Illinois College had a medical department which, along with Rush Medical College in Chicago, was one of the first two medical schools in Illinois; this department of the college was abolished when it became difficult to pay professional salaries in cash and when the anatomy question had become a divisive one in medical circles.

All of these organizations and institutions were founded in a town which at no time during the period referred to had a population of over 12,000, and until the 1860s was much smaller. It was no mere touch of civic pride, therefore, which gave Jacksonville the title of "The Athens of the West," a term by which it came to be known far from the Illinois prairie by which it was surrounded. Just when this term originated is uncertain, but it was definitely in vogue by the 1850s. It is possible that the term was first used by the families who early emigrated from Huntsville, Alabama, at the time a town which had many of the cultural character- istics of Jacksonville and which had been called "The Athens of the South." It may have been brought along by emigrants from Lexington, Kentucky, which had on occasion also been referred to as "The Athens of the West" or it may have been applied by Alcott, Emerson, and other visitors from the East. In any case, the term "The Athens of the West" was not inappropriate.[1]

There was a fairly large influx of southern people during the early decades of Jacksonville's history. This precipitated a bitter controversy over the issue of slavery and only the definite preponderance of a northern element kept the battle within bounds. The educational institutions were largely administered by people who had come from the East. The establishment of Illinois College was finally consummated by the famous "Yale Band" which played such a significant part in the westward march of higher education. Edward Beecher, the first president, was the son of Lyman Beecher ; his successor, Julian M. Sturtevant, was a Yale graduate. The first principal of the Jacksonville Female Academy was Sarah C. Crocker, who was chosen on the recommendation of Mary Lyon, the mother of higher education for women in the United States. A later principal of the same institu- tion was a John Adams, who went to Jacksonville from the

---

[1] Jacksonville was not the only town to lay claim to this title, how- ever. St. Louis, Crawfordsville, Indiana, Iowa City, Iowa, Topeka and Emporia, Kansas were others which at one time or another appropriated it, although none of them had the same justification for so doing as Jacksonville and none was so commonly identified by the title.

headship of Phillips Academy in Andover. A list of the educational leaders of the community would indicate a decided leaning toward New England in the choice of candidates.

Jacksonville never succumbed to the industrial wave which accompanied the advance of scientific invention. From the beginning it was self-contained, with an abundant supply of academic and corrective institutions. Its character was to be determined by these, not very largely by the ebb and flow of economic forces. Not that Jacksonville had no concern over economic problems; it was concerned, both in terms of the difficulties of keeping the private institutions alive and in terms of its dependence upon the surrounding agricultural territory. Fortunately, however, the latter made of Jacksonville an important center for business and banking, and the institutions came to be more adequately cared for as the wealth of the community increased and benefactors elsewhere made their contributions. The economic life of Jacksonville became stabilized earlier than that of other towns of its size, leaving more time for the pursuit of cultural aims. The institutions it housed provided much of the material and set the tempo for its culture. The very nature of its life made Jacksonville ready soil for the cultivation of philosophy. This interest took organized form in 1860 and continued for over thirty years, making it possible for William Torrey Harris to write in 1890, "Jacksonville is a sort of university city for philosophy in this country, and we are all interested in its doings, that is to say, all of us who are interested in philosophy." [2]

The influence of Dr. Hiram K. Jones was an important factor in the development of philosophy in Jacksonville.

[2] Letter to Louise M. Fuller, November 21, 1890, *Journal of the American Akademe,* 5 (1890) 18.

Jacksonville without Jones would probably never have produced a Platonic circle just as Jones without Jacksonville could hardly have established such a continuous and expansive circle. We have dealt with one side of this partnership; it now remains to turn to Jones, to see what contribution he made to the culture of this "Athens of the West." His influence was more than casual, it was contagious; so contagious, in fact, that he came to be referred to as the "Western Metaphysical Giant," the "Western Wonder," and the "Modern Plato."

The American ancestry of Jones can be traced back to the days of the Revolution, his paternal grandfather having emigrated to this country and later having served directly under General Washington in the Revolutionary Army, a fact of which Jones was eminently proud. He was born in Culpepper, Virginia, August 5, 1818, the son of Stephen and Mildred Jones. When Jones was nine, he had his first taste of the West when the family settled at Troy, Missouri, where his father engaged in farming. He remained at home until he was sixteen, during which time he had not only secured his own preliminary education but had already begun to teach. Altogether, he had taught eight years in elementary school before, at the comparatively late age of twenty-two, he set out for Jacksonville to enter Illinois College. In 1844 he finished the classical course with honors and continued on for three more years during which he received the M.D. (1846) and M.A. (1847) degrees. He then returned home (now, Ashley, Missouri) to practice medicine, and not long afterward met and married Elizabeth Orr, whose father, Philip Orr, was a judge. The marriage was a happy one, for Mrs. Jones (familiarly known as Lizzie) was as much interested in Dr. Jones' professional and philosophical career as he, her own philosophical talent was far above the average, and she came to be an influential member of the Platonic circle. Whether Jones' practice failed to materialize as he thought it should or whether the more cultured city of Jacksonville was the primary attraction is difficult to say; in either case, the Joneses moved to Jacksonville in the early 1850s. In 1854 Jones served as acting superintendent of the Hospital for the Insane, but upon the permanent appointment of a new head for the institution he returned to private practice, which he continued until his death on June 16, 1903, probably caused by a growing frequency of nocturnal epilepsy.

As a medical practitioner, Jones was regarded highly, particularly in the early years of his career. He did not even bother to put a shingle out until after thirty years, and then the fact that a woman patient from abroad had hunted for the office in the hot sun, until she nearly fainted from exhaustion, led him to conclude that it was good sense to let the public be informed of his place of practice. Various stories are told of him as a doctor, from his frequent use of psychiatric techniques (perhaps traceable to his experience with the insane) to his dirty, somewhat stained vest which seems to have impressed the young quite as much as his large "pill-box" with whose contents he sought to effect cures.

His technique was probably above the average for his day, his procedure, conventional. He followed the eclectic school in medicine, employing vegetable compounds in treatment, hoping by this means to conserve the energy of the patient until the normal process of recovery had taken place. He was one of the founders of the local Microscopic Society and brought back from Europe valuable equipment which he used in his demonstrations at Illinois College and made available to other physicians. Still, he came to oppose the germ theory, and his eclipse as a physician, at least as far as the younger members of the profession were concerned, came when he read a paper in February, 1890, before the local medical society entitled "The Anatomy and Physiology of Micro-Organisms" in which he rejected the new theory. The paper was much criticized, and after this he never regained stature among his colleagues. His philosophical pursuits doubtless prevented him from keeping abreast of developments in his profession and hence led to his being regarded locally as a "man of the old school." Whatever the criticism of his medical knowledge, he nevertheless had, and kept, a large practice, remunerative to the extent that he could become a large benefactor of his alma mater in his later years.

As a citizen, Jones was held in high regard. In addition to being a founder of the Microscopic Society, he was a charter member of the Literary Society, and gave time and effort to all worthy public enterprises. He was a loyal alumnus of Illinois College, serving as president of its board of trustees for ten years. He lectured on anatomy and physiology intermittently there, from 1886 to 1900. He was interested in the maintenance of a deer park close to Jacksonville and kept a log of all the artesian wells in the vicinity as an avocation as well as a public service. He was a Republican in politics, a friend and supporter of Lincoln, and on one occasion, because of his strong antislavery sentiments, campaigned for a seat in the legislature. He was friendly to students, particularly to those who found the economic struggle difficult, permitting some, among them William Jennings Bryan, to live in his home. His philanthropy was largely directed toward Illinois College. In 1895 he gave $20,000 for a new chapel and library. He was to receive an annuity from this but shortly thereafter waived the privilege. The building was dedicated in 1897 as Jones Hall, in memory of his wife; at the ceremony the program was philosophical, with addresses by James H. Tufts on "The Development of Individuality and Individualism," by William Torrey Harris on "The Fruits of Philosophy," and by Jones on "Philosophy in Higher Education." In 1902 he gave another $10,000 and his will provided an additional $38,-000 for endowment. By these bequests he became the greatest single alumni benefactor of the college. His library was also given to the college, but it is difficult to determine just how many books were included because they have now been assimilated into the regular college collection.[3]

Jones, the family doctor, and Jones the citizen and benefactor, will never achieve the position of eminence which Jones, the Platonic philosopher, did. In philosophy, contrary to the tradition which was beginning to take hold during his life, Jones was largely self-made. Like his contemporaries in St. Louis, Jones regarded philosophy as a necessary orientation for the whole business of human living. It gave impetus to vocational pursuits and it enriched the leisure hours. It brought the tangled miscellany of human experience into some semblance of harmony, providing meaning and purpose.

Jones' philosophical interest began while he was in college. Emerson was the chief object of his attention at the time, not because of, but in spite of, any instruction which he received. This is the story in his own words:

> When I was a student in Illinois College there were two other students and myself who got hold of Emerson's writings. Of course we were ridiculed for dabbling in such transcendental non-

[3] An account of Jones' life is included here because only one other account is available and that relatively inaccessible. It is an obituary written by T. J. Pitner, C. E. Black, and F. P. Norbury and is printed in *The Illinois Medical Journal,* 5 (1903–4), 173–74.

sense. These writings were then denounced on all sides. We continued to read Emerson. Now within one short lifetime that thought has conquered and subdued all minds. The power of this thought has created a receptivity for ideas.[4]

Emerson obviously awakened Jones to the possibilities of philosophical study. But, like most students, Jones was not satisfied to equate philosophy with the thought of one philosopher, and this acquaintance with Emerson came to be for him but an introduction to a whole world of new meaning, a world with which he became increasingly familiar as the years rolled by, though a world which still retained some of the overtones which his first real teacher provided for him. Upon his graduation he feared that this new discovery might slip from his hands, but he quickly came to the realization that the decision remained with him. He records the experience in the following words:

I was walking across the hill after my graduation full of regret that school days were over. The thought of dropping all the lines of delightful study I had been pursuing, filled me with melancholy: there seemed no interest in the future equal to that I was leaving. Suddenly it occurred to me that I might *still be a student;* that I need not *give up study.* From that moment all was clear, and I may indeed say that I have been a student all my life.[5]

The respect with which Jones regarded Emerson never diminished, but he was unsatisfied until he began to drink from the same philosophical font which had fortified his guide, the whole Platonic tradition from Plato to Thomas Taylor. One of Jones' followers [6] referred to him as wearing the mantle of Dr. Tayler Lewis and it is perhaps true that

[4] *Journal of the American Akademe,* III (1887), 171.
[5] *Ibid.,* V (1890), 18.
[6] "Viator," who defended Jones and the Plato Club in the local paper in the fall of 1879 from the cynical jests of local punsters.

Lewis did have an inspirational effect upon Jones, but he hardly influenced him to the extent indicated. Lewis was a classical scholar of considerable importance who taught at New York University and Union College. His one book on Plato, *Plato against the Atheists*, which came out in 1845, was a running commentary on the tenth book of the *Laws*. Its main object was to dispel, invoking the authority of Plato, tendencies at the time which he regarded as atheistic. He conceived the tenth book of the *Laws* to be the best introduction to Plato's system as a whole, but the book was not so much intended to be an introduction to Plato as to be a refutation of atheism. It is true that Lewis and Jones did have some points in common, such as their desire to provide an antidote to the inductive method of reasoning which they regarded as responsible for the "materialistic" emphasis of the day, but a comparison of the approach of the two men to Plato is alone sufficient to discount Lewis' influence on Jones. Lewis made the *Laws* the key to the whole Platonic system while Jones regarded the *Laws* as spurious. Furthermore, there is no evidence that the men ever had contact with each other, through correspondence or personal acquaintance. Jones undoubtedly read Lewis' book, but it is doubtful if this had other than an inspirational effect upon his own development of a Platonic philosophy. What really influenced Jones more than anything else was the reading of Plato himself, a project upon which he was engaged in earnest by the early 1860s. What he did in a philosophical way during the late 1840s and 1850s is difficult to determine, but it is doubtful if he did much more than occasional reading during this period, as he probably was engaged sufficiently in establishing his medical practice to prevent any thorough philosophical research.

One factor which encouraged Jones in his study of philosophy was the uncertainty in medical circles at the time concerning basic principles. This led Jones to seek some undergirding for his medicine in philosophical concepts. J. J. Garth Wilkinson, well-known English surgeon and homeopathist who edited Swedenborg's works, had provided such a basis for his own medicine in his *Human Body and its Connection with Man* (London, 1851; second edition, 1860), in which he argued that the nervous system was a sort of physical handle of the spirit, providing a link between the spirit and the body; for this he was indebted to Swedenborg. Jones became interested in this book, although it is difficult to say how seriously he followed Wilkinson. When he started the Plato Club in 1865 he was talking about Wilkinson, and the fact that Alexander Wilder, another physician, could present a paper on Wilkinson before the American Akademe as late as 1891, indicates that Wilkinson had not been lost sight of during the intervening period. It is probable, however, that this influence was little more than another incentive for Jones to seek a Platonic synthesis of his own as well as provide a brief introduction to Swedenborg. While Jones did find in Platonism a system for relating the mind and the body, he never completely readjusted his medical practice to conform to it. Evidence of this is to be found in the discussion which followed his paper on "Man and His Material Body," which he read before the American Akademe in November, 1890. In this Jones had argued that the body was passive, without form and without life in itself. Elizur Wolcott, who invariably proved to be a critic of Jones' position, asked Jones what he would do if he (Wolcott) took sick in the night and asked Jones to call; he answered his own question by saying, "You know very well what he will do; he will come with his *case of medicines* and do his utmost to change the material conditions that are tormenting me." Jones then retorted, perhaps facetiously or perhaps in self defense, "I would ask you what you had been doing," to which Wolcott replied, "No; you would work away with your pills trying to hit that point of actual distress occasioned by some misplaced matter." [7] Jones certainly found his Platonism satisfactory for religious and moral purposes but he never completely adapted his medicine to it. This is another way of saying that Jones wanted more than an explanation for medicine; he wanted a point of view which would harmonize man's physical, moral, intellectual, and religious needs. His medicine increasingly became a means of living, his philosophy reason for it.

When Jones first took up the serious reading of Plato in 1860 his enthusiasm was hard to keep within bounds. Whenever friends of his showed the least interest in philosophical problems he trotted out his new-found bible and read passages to them. It was not long until he had made three permanent converts to his new course of study, Miss Louise Fuller, Mrs. J. O. King, and Mrs. Elizur Wolcott. They agreed to meet every Saturday morning for the reading of the Platonic dialogues and for discussion suggested by them. Saturday morning proved to be a wise choice of time for these meetings for, as the group grew, people in education joined it, and for them, this was obviously convenient. At first the meetings were held at Mrs. Wolcott's home, then at Mrs. King's, followed by changes to the homes of Miss Anna Paxson and others, and finally to Jones' study, which became a more permanent place of meeting.

Mrs. Wolcott, writing in 1890, threw some light on the psychological origin of this Plato Club, although she un-

[7] *Journal of the American Akademe,* V (1890), 56.

doubtedly overestimated the bitterness of the struggle involved. She said,

One summer morning thirty years ago, three friends met in an upper chamber, to decide how they might best inaugurate a plan which should serve once a week to draw them away from the absorbing cares of every-day life, and elevate them to some purer realm from whose heights life in all its interests might appear in its true relations, and where mind and heart might be so strengthened and sweetened that the toil and stress of life's battle might be more easily and courageously borne.[8]

It hardly seems likely that the three ladies concerned found life quite as tiresome as the last sentence of this quotation would indicate, for they had no economic problems and they were among the leading women of the city, but the quotation does suggest that resident in their minds was a psychological and intellectual need that had not been satisfied otherwise. They talked at first about reading the Bible and then, after conferring with Hiram K. Jones, concluded that Plato was probably the fountain at which they wished to drink. Thus the Plato Club came into existence, not to lose its influence until the 1890s.

At first the meetings consisted of reading and discussing the dialogues, but, as Jones became more thoroughly acquainted with Plato and the organization grew in size, the meetings took on the character of a group interested in the gospel of Plato as interpreted by H. K. Jones. Sections of a dialogue would be read and then Jones would interpret the meaning. The plan was more that of a German institu-

---

[8] "The Plato Club of Jacksonville, Illinois," *Bibliotheca Platonica*, I (1890), 287. This is one of the three accounts of the Plato Club written by members. The other two are by Louis Block and Miss Louise Fuller; they appeared respectively in *The Platonist*, I (1881), 84–85, and in *Journal of the American Akademe*, V (1890), 18–24.

tion of higher learning than that of Plato. As Miss Fuller coyly remarked, "In type of mind Dr. Jones is unlike Plato, and still less like Socrates. In the Club things are laid down with no uncertain sound; discipline,—tolerable." [9] On the whole the members did not seem to resent the presentation of truth from on high and came to look upon Jones as a philosopher in his own right and as such a man to whom it was worth listening. There was discussion, of course, and there were some who were bold enough to question Jones both on his interpretation of Plato and on his own ideas, but he clearly held the center of the stage as well as the respect of all. The Bohn translation was used for the most part, but other translations and the original Greek were referred to when further clarity on disputed points was desired. In the course of the three decades of the club's existence, the dialogues, with the exception of the *Laws*, were read through twice, some a third time, and others were studied more often. The *Charmides* was the first dialogue read and confirms the statement that Jones wished some philosophical basis for his medicine, since it dealt largely with health and medicine. From that point on, however, the other dialogues such as the *Republic*, the *Timaeus*, and the *Symposium* took first place in the affection of the members. Notes on the readings and comments were taken by Mrs. King and sent to Mrs. Sarah Denman in Quincy where they were used in the meetings of the early Plato group in that city. After Mrs. King's death Mrs. Wolcott continued to take notes, some of which were published in *The Journal of Speculative Philosophy* and elsewhere.[10]

[9] *Journal of the American Akademe*, V (1890), 22.
[10] What remains of Mrs. King's notes is in the possession of Mrs. Albert E. McVitty of Princeton, N.J. These are practically identical with the notes of Mrs. Denman, referred to later. See p. 134 below.

The first influx of new members was from the ranks of local teachers and included Mrs. Charles Drury, Miss Anna Paxson, Miss Mary Selby, and Miss Elizabeth Wright. They were regarded as excellent additions because it was felt that, as educators, they brought with them a regard for study combined with an eye for its fruitful results.

The second group which was admitted in the early 1870s, also largely of teachers, included D. H. Harris, brother of William Torrey Harris, and Louis J. Block, whom Harris, as superintendent of the Jacksonville schools, brought to Jacksonville to become principal of the high school. With these two men, particularly with Block, a wave of Hegelian philosophy came in. Harris at this time was not actively aligned with his brother's movement in St. Louis, although he knew about it and had natural sympathies with it. Block, on the other hand, had been an associate member of the group in St. Louis and provided a fresh approach which he had acquired while there. As for the later inclination of these men, Harris moved more decidedly in the direction of Hegelianism and later became closely associated with Denton J. Snider in the Communal University in St. Louis, while Block transferred his major allegiance from Hegel to Plato and became an important leader both in the Plato Club and in The American Akademe. Harris left Jacksonville around 1880 because of the ill-health of his wife and Block moved to Chicago the next year. But in any event, the Hegelian point of view never threatened the supremacy of Plato in the minds of the local people.[11] The "Athens of the West" remained loyal to its epithet.

It would be a mistake, however, to think of the Plato Club

---

[11] An H. M. Jones was a member of the St. Louis Philosophical Society but there is no evidence that this was Hiram K. Jones.

as an organization whose sole function was the understanding and glorification of Plato in any esoteric sense. Jones himself was a man of wide reading both in philosophy and literature; he was constantly associating ideas in Plato with similar ones in Dante, Shakespeare, Goethe, Spenser, and others and drawing parallels in Christian, Hindu, Persian, and Chinese thought. Members of the club had specific allegiances of their own and they were free to interpret Plato as they saw fit. There was no credal basis for membership, nor were there religious or racial discriminations. Elizur Wolcott, a devotee of science, defended the doctrine of evolution although Jones and others did not accept either its Darwinian or Spencerian interpretations. Mrs. Ellen Ramsey was a champion of Swedenborg and introduced his philosophy whenever possible. Block, a Jew and a religious independent, was listened to as attentively as anyone. The members not only represented different points of view but they had widely diverse interests, despite the fact that the early membership was composed largely of teachers and a goodly number of them were included, even when their proportion dropped.

The club did not lack interest from the standpoint of the variety of attitudes and inclinations involved. One member easily burst forth with spontaneous intuitive insights whenever the spirit called her. Another, a staunch Presbyterian, liked Plato as well as the others, but always kept an eye peeled for signs of heresy. There were others whose denominational affiliations were nominal and this permitted them to say and think almost anything which seemed reasonable. One member flowered forth with pertinent bits of poetry whenever occasion permitted. Another had a ready streak of humor to lighten the discussion when it became too heated or involved. The group ranged in attitude from those who took their philosophy no more seriously than anything else to those who moved to Jacksonville for the express purpose of philosophical enlightenment. What distinguished the Plato Club from other organizations in the Midwest at the time was not so much the variety of people involved as their continuous devotion to a club whose primary purpose was the study of Plato's dialogues. For Jones, the variety of ideas and attitudes symbolized the plural expressions of the universal truth of Plato. Plato, for Jones, was sufficiently catholic to embrace in his point of view all of the lesser truths expounded under a thousand different names and in behalf of many different systems.[12]

The Plato Club was largely a Jacksonville organization but its influence spread and it attracted visitors from nearby cities such as Quincy and others as far away as Davenport, Iowa. It sought stimulation from outside, too. In addition to Bronson Alcott's "conversations," Denton J. Snider spoke on Hegel, Shakespeare, and Goethe, W. T. Harris on Hegel, and Thomas Davidson on Aristotle, and H. H. Morgan, editor of *The Western*, and Thomas M. Johnson of Osceola, Missouri were visitors. These voices, however, were but eddies in a stream, ultimately conquered by the main flow of Platonic ideology as it came from the dialogues of Plato, and was distilled by Hiram K. Jones.

The effect of the Plato Club varied somewhat with the

[12] No record of the complete membership of the club is available. The following is a partial list in addition to those already mentioned: the Mesdames H. K. Jones, Julia Palmer Stevens, Alexander McDonald, I. L. Morrison, M. J. Kellogg, M. J. Stearns, Mary Kirk, and D. H. Harris; the Misses Mary King, Emma King, Edith Wolcott, Jennie Meek, Mary Rhoads, Sarah Allen; Messrs. Charles Drury, Chauncey Carter, E. E. Butler, William Clark, a Mr. Clayton, and a Mr. Wendte. A large portion of the membership was women.

interests of the members. The attitudes of the three who have written accounts of the club are perhaps representative. Miss Fuller, who was not only a member of the Plato Club but a leader in the American Akademe and editor of the last two volumes of its *Journal*, regarded the club as a means of general education. Plato, for her, was a window through which to see and understand the world's great literature and philosophy. Her attention was always focused on the practical results of thought, and Plato was a means for enriching personal and social life as well, presenting, as he did, a scheme of thought which brought the minutiae of life into perspective. For Mrs. Wolcott, Plato served religious purposes, for he presented a vision of the eternality of truth as distinguished from the transitoriness of temporal relations. While she held that Plato never achieved a system which attained to mathematical or logical completion, she did feel he sketched a method and embodied an attitude which encouraged men to seek unity and intrinsic good. The almost mystic quality of her writing sums up this particular type of reaction.

Having walked with him in pursuit of some ideal form, we can never again be as ignorant of its nature as before, for his clear vision chases away the darkness of ignorance and opens vistas in every direction as he goes on, at last leading us to those heights from whose summits new truth becomes visible, new light breaks in on us, and we plant our stakes further out in the Infinite than ever before.[13]

A third type of reaction was represented by Louis Block, who recognized the educational and the religious value in Plato but who, even more, regarded Plato as the founder of a system; a system in which not all elements were carefully

[13] *Bibliotheca Platonica,* I (1890), 289–90.

organized but whose main outline was clearly apparent. He regarded the Plato Club as a Platonic school where the essential ingredients of that system could be studied and learned. His view of what the Plato Club taught can be summed up in a few sentences. There existed a first creator, understood best as absolute energy. The creator produced a whole hierarchy of being in which man was the center, above were the various orders of sub-deities, and below were spheres antagonistic to the good. The universe was a reflection of the first cause, a dimming of its power and goodness. The human realm was that in which the created prepared for a return to its source. The soul, the connecting link, was resident in the body for purposes of experience leading to purification, the achievement of which would culminate in reunion with the creator. The procedure was rational, for only through knowledge of truth could the soul find its way back to its eternal haven. Truth, however, was not so much an aggregate of facts to be apprehended as it was a way of life to be understood and followed.[14]

The Plato Club served a variety of functions for its members, and if they and they alone had been involved it would still be a story worth recording. But it was more than that; it was a cell from which a larger organism developed. The Plato Club was the beginning of a movement which spread its influence beyond the limited cultural environs of Jacksonville to other cities such as Quincy, Decatur, and Bloomington, to the larger public which Jones, as its spokesman, addressed at the Concord School of Philosophy, and to the still larger public which read the *Journal of the American Akademe*. The Plato Club was Jones' training ground, for, despite his somewhat oracular and doctrinaire commentaries

[14] Refer to *The Platonist*, I (1881), 84–85.

on the dialogues, he found there a group of people of serious intent and broad experience who served to polish his thought and eradicate its weaknesses through questions, comments, and criticism. It was no mere freak of nature, therefore, which brought Jones to the fore and made it possible for him to be regarded as the leading Platonic teacher in the country.

It has already been remarked that Jones was one of the chief figures in the Concord School of Philosophy. The founding of this school was due to the strength of philosophy in the Midwest. Newspapers often spoke of it as a triumph of midwestern culture. Certainly Jones, along with his Platonic followers, did much to make a success of the school, as a quotation or two will quickly show. A writer in the Detroit *Free Press* said: "The strong cards of the party are Alcott, Harris and Jones, . . . If you never heard of Jones you had better say you never heard of Plato and confess yourself an ignoramus at once.[15]

Something of the light in which Jones' lectures were viewed is indicated by a statement appearing in the Boston *Evening Traveller* along with a report of Jones' lecture on Platonic psychology:

Dr. Jones' lectures are a very pronounced feature of the Concord School. They are felt to be a wonderful insight into Platonian philosophy, an exposition of mysticism, that is clear, vital and forcible. They impress people. They inspire almost infinite suggestion and speculation, and a "Plato morning," as we had today, naturally attracts a very critical and interested audience. Dr. Jones has a certain *clientele* who hang upon his words, so to speak, and who regard his thought as a very remarkable system

[15] Included in scrapbook of "Aunt Biddie," pen-name for Mrs. Hiram K. Jones, who kept a record of her visits to the Concord School. This is to be found in the Illinois College Library.

of philosophy. This fact is also true of the west. The writer has personally known of people going to the town where Dr. Jones lives—Jacksonville, Ill.—and staying days simply to hear Dr. Jones talk. The Doctor is a tall, straight, alert man, with the silvered hair of the sage, the cool, deep blue eyes of the thinker, the fire and vigor of youth. A straightforward, courteous gentleman, ready with his words, not afraid to speak the truth as it is in Emerson, a man who *practicalizes* his mysticism, if I may so express it; that is, he does not talk vapors, but he talks good sense.[16]

It is reported that one enthusiastic student of Jones said that under his influence even the elms seemed straighter and taller than they did anywhere else. Yet Jones was neither a literary genius nor a news reporter of philosophical truth. Condensation was no virtue of his, and many of his listeners would find five hours of one of his lectures trying on the mind and hence stay for an hour or so, then go out for air and return for more. Lilian Whiting records such attitudes in a very enlightening manner, indicating something of the quality of Jones' fare as well.

Sometimes, indeed, an irreverent couple would leave these Platonic expositions of the "physical sensorium" and "spiritual sensoria" and be off for an hour's row on the Concord River,—whose current is so sluggish that Hawthorne said he swam across it every day all one summer without being able to determine which way it flowed,—but as the lectures of Dr. Jones were, like the quality of Japanese pictures, such as to permit approach from any angle of vision,—upside down, or divided anywhere; any part, despite mathematical laws, being equal to the whole,—they lent themselves to the charming possibilities of being taken in sections. Indeed, the irreverent and unplatonic mind was not unfrequently found to insist that a part was better than the whole of the good doctor's discourses, whose length suggested the

[16] *Ibid.* n.d.

infinite leisure of the eternities rather than the limits of an ephemeral summer's day.[17]

The first four years of the Concord School witnessed a friendly, but sometimes frictional, debate between Hegel and Plato, as represented by Harris and Jones. After the fourth session Jones never appeared again at the school. Part of the explanation for this lies in the fact that Hegel seemed to be getting the better of Plato, at least so Denton J. Snider tells us. However, this might be somewhat discounted, since Snider was largely Hegelian in his own thinking. The fact also that Harris and Jones retained their friendship long after this occasion casts discredit on the complete validity of Snider's thesis. It is more likely that the argument over where the school should subsequently be held is what alienated Jones. The people from the Midwest argued that it should be transferred to that section of the country because it had supplied such a large proportion of the attendants.[18] How much Jones led in this movement is hard to say but he was certainly in favor of the transfer and obviously very disappointed when it was decided to continue the school in Concord. The fact that Jones never returned to Concord and that he started the American Akademe in Jacksonville the following year is adequate evidence of where

[17] *Boston Days: The City of Beautiful Ideals, Concord and its Famous Authors, the Golden Age of Genius, Dawn of the Twentieth Century* (Boston, Little Brown, 1902), p. 175.

[18] There was evidently quite a debate over this issue at the close of the 1882 session. Alcott wrote: "The attendants at our school are largely from the West, and we have entertained the thought of holding a session of the school at some acceptable and wholesome resort in those parts. Doubtless the attendance would be largely increased and the school advertised by this transfer for a session. But it has seemed, however desirable it might prove to westerners, to be the policy to continue the school at the chapel as heretofore. Concord and Concord only is the proper seat of the school and so we shall announce tomorrow." MS, Diary for 1882, August 11.

his feeling was. When Jones left the school it suffered greatly, for his going meant the loss of the major figure in the Platonic element, leaving the field open for the eclipse of Platonism by Hegelianism. This had further effect in that the lack of adequate competition for the Hegelian group lessened the intensity of philosophical discussion, and it soon gave way to a literary interest.

All of these events had their natural effect upon what followed. As the Plato Club and other such organizations were instrumental in the founding of the Concord School, so the break away from the Concord School was a powerful incentive for the formation of the American Akademe the following year in Jacksonville. The Akademe was not a summer school, for the heat of central Illinois during that time of the year would have been no aid in attracting people to Jacksonville. It was a wise move, therefore, to make the Akademe a permanent winter organization with monthly meetings, instead. The plan of meeting intermittently although regularly had another value, that of not wearing the members out, as the Concord School had a tendency to do. The nucleus was the Plato Club, which was still operating and was to continue to do so even after the Akademe had ceased to exist; nevertheless, the organization was not solely a Jacksonville one even from the start, and its Platonism, while decidedly influential, was not oppressive.

The American Akademe came into being as a result of a meeting held in Jacksonville on July 2, 1883. Jones presided, and Alexander Wilder, of Newark, New Jersey, whom Jones had met at Concord two years earlier and with whom he had much in common, acted as secretary. According to the records of the organization, "The presiding officer explained the purpose of the meeting to be to take the necessary preliminary steps for forming a permanent organization of individuals desiring to pursue and promote Philosophic enquiry." [19] There were thirty-three people present, of whom twenty-one were from Jacksonville and the remainder from elsewhere in the country, from Galveston to New York City. The list included in addition to Jones and Wilder, Louise M. Fuller (who later edited the Journal of the American Akademe), Thomas M. Johnson, editor of *The Platonist*, and W. T. Harris and Block, both of whom appeared at Concord to lecture later in the summer. The fact that Harris appeared for this meeting and later read papers before the group or had them read for him is a testimony to his interest in seeing the philosophic urge continued in the Midwest even though his own residence had been changed to Concord.

At this first meeting a committee was appointed to prepare a plan of organization. The committee reported on September 25 of the same year and a constitution was read and approved. Eighteen new members were elected, including the publishers A. W. Wagnalls and Abner Doubleday of New York, and others from Colorado to the Dutch West Indies. Officers elected for a period of three years at this meeting were Dr. Hiram K. Jones, president; Dr. Alexander Wilder, vice president; Mrs. Julia P. Stevens, recording secretary; and Thomas M. Johnson, Louis J. Block and Mrs. B. Paxson Drury, corresponding secretaries. The reason for the corresponding secretaries was that the organization had a policy of encouraging comments, letters, and contributions. How extensive this particular task became is not easy to determine but the fact that minutes of meetings

---

[19] MS, "Records of the American Akademe," p. 3. These are in the Illinois College Library.

constantly carried references to the comments sent in by members and to the relatively few which could actually be read at any one meeting would seem to indicate a rather extensive mail department.

The name of the organization was probably suggested by Wilder, for he had argued in Concord the previous summer that if the Concord School wished to be permanent it ought to change its name to "The Akademe." It is also of interest to know that Alcott had suggested "The New Academy" as an appropriate title for the Concord School before it was actually established. It seemed quite natural, therefore, to choose the name for the Jacksonville organization which had been suggested for the Concord School, since these people regarded the American Akademe as the successor of that school.

The purpose of the organization as defined in the constitution was "to promote the knowledge of philosophic truth, and to co-operate in the dissemination of such knowledge, with a view to the elevation of the mind from the sphere of the sensuous life into that of virtue and justice, and into communion with the diviner ideas and natures." The organization was nonsectarian, yet there was a bond of unity in the Platonic interest which most of them shared and which Jones was so instrumental in furthering. An oft-repeated statement of many of the group was that the Akademe was "a School rather than a sect in philosophy, with personal improvement and the intellection of Truth as the ulterior purpose," and while in general this was true, no one doubted the diffusive effect of the Platonic background of the organization and of most of its members. When the atmosphere wasn't specifically Platonic it was at least antimaterialistic. These people were well aware of the growing influence of the

scientific mind in the nineteenth century as it expressed itself in physical and biological studies. They were equally
aware of the growing importance of economics in a civilization that was becoming more and more industrial. They
were not so much opposed to this "brave new world" as they
were afraid that in it some of the cherished values of the
past might be lost, and it was those values for which they
wished to find adequate defense. Thomas M. Johnson gave a
fair estimate of the framework in which the Akademe should
be viewed when he said:

Already there is manifest among individuals of various shades
of opinion in the thinking world, something like a reacting impulse against the materialism of the age, to arrest its progress
before it shall totally benumb the moral sense of mankind. The
modest little assemblages of late years, such as the School of
Philosophy at Concord, the School of Christian Philosophy at
Greenwood Lake, and other places, and the various organizations
of other forms, but all seeking to direct attention to a higher and
more practical spirituality, are so many witnesses. The American
Akademe, latest of them all with a Plato Club for its nucleus,
and a goodly number, steadily increasing, of earnest, clear-seeing
men and women for its membership, also voices the same conclusion.

With many criticisms of its heretical orthodoxy, and its immaterial view of evolution, the Akademe holds on its way repre-
senting many schools of thought and various beliefs, yet true to
the discipline of cooperative effort in speculative research.[20]

More must be said about the "heretical orthodoxy" of
which Johnson spoke, but for the present let us return to
certain other considerations about the organization and the
members who composed it. Although the constitution was
approved in September and a meeting was held in October

[20] *The Platonist*, II (1884), 1.

to take in another large group of applicants for membership, it was not until December, 1883, that the first complete program was presented. At this meeting it was decided that the third Tuesday of each month would be the date for meeting and that ten meetings would be held each year, from September to June. These early meetings were held in Dr. Jones' study but it soon became apparent that more commodious quarters would have to be found. The result was that Jones turned over a large upstairs room in his home and this came to be known as Akademe Hall. It was bare except for linoleum on the floor and chairs around the walls, as if to indicate an intention to provide nothing which would distract from thought, the central object of their common quest.

It was agreed that at each meeting a paper would be read, after which discussion of its merits would follow. The record of these discussions, at least such of it as has been preserved, indicates that while gentility was always the order of the day, frankness and candor were not lacking. Membership rapidly increased until in May, 1884, there were 180 members. When the last meeting was held in 1892 there had been 433 members enrolled, although probably no more than 200 were members at any one time. There is no way of validating this statement because the roll was cumulative and resignations were not recorded. From the standpoint of the number enrolled, it can certainly be said that the Akademe surpassed the St. Louis Movement and it compared favorably with the Concord School, which never had that number enrolled in any one year. From the standpoint of its permanent influence, at least in the field of philosophy, it can hardly compare with the St. Louis Movement, particularly when the *Journal of Speculative Philosophy* is taken into account, although it probably exceeded in this regard the Concord School, which came more and more to take on the character of a short summer chautauqua whose audience was sporadic and often motivated by other than purely intellectual interests.

The average attendance at meetings of the Akademe during the first few years was somewhere around fifty, but by 1890 it had begun to fall off until in the last few months it went down to thirty. Part of the gap between membership and attendance is to be explained by the fact that about one-third of the membership was from outside Jacksonville and many of them had never attended a meeting. Members were enrolled from all over the world. Hull, England; Sydney, New South Wales; Paris, France; and Uzulman, Mexico were but four of the cities from which foreign members were enrolled, and as far as the United States was concerned, members were found from coast to coast. Jones made no idle remark in 1884 when he said, "This is not a *local* but a continental association; . . . its aim is, to find out persons of kindred thought and appreciation; . . . its membership extends from Maine to California, and from Canada to the West Indies, and . . . we shall continue to maintain its continental character." [21]

Still, of course, the majority of the members were Jacksonville residents, giving the organization a natural nucleus for solidarity and permanence.

Whereas the Plato Club had a preponderance of feminine members, the American Akademe had a more nearly equal distribution of the sexes. It also drew its members from a more inclusive circle. There was a strikingly large number of physicians: H. K. Jones, C. G. Jones, T. J. Pitner, J. R.

[21] MS, "Records of the American Akademe," p. 25.

Sutherland, David Prince, G. V. Black and A. H. Kellogg, all of Jacksonville, as well as Alexander Wilder of Newark, George Winterburn of New York (editor of the *American Homeopathist*), Samuel Willard of Chicago (who had given up medicine for teaching history), and C. A. Lindorme of Fort Reed, Florida. The local institutions of higher learning were well represented with President E. A. Tanner and Professors Harvey W. Milligan, J. B. Turner, E. F. Bullard, and J. William Pattison from Illinois College, and Presidents William F. Short and Joseph R. Harker of Illinois Women's College (MacMurray College). College professors from Colorado, Toronto, Albion, Bethany and Buchtel (Akron University) were also enrolled. There was a moderate number of ministers, among whom were C. F. Bradley of Quincy, a Mr. Eby of Peoria, William M. Campbell of Carrollton, A. B. Morey, W. N. McElroy, F. S. Hayden and J. T. McFarland, of Jacksonville. Women who took a particularly prominent part in the organization were Mrs. Julia P. Stevens and Mrs. B. Paxson Drury, both corresponding secretaries, Sadie G. Hamilton and Emily Wing, secretaries, Louise M. Fuller, Mrs. Elizur Wolcott, and Mrs. Helen Campbell. The St. Louis group was represented by W. T. Harris, Denton J. Snider and Louis Soldan. Other influential members of particular interest were Thomas M. Johnson, whose *Platonist* and *Bibliotheca Platonica* were important in their own right, J. Barthelemy St. Hilaire of Paris, C. H. A. Bjerregard, head of the Astor Library in New York City, Louis Block of Chicago, and S. H. Emery, Jr. and Edward McClure of Quincy and Concord. This incomplete list of members indicates that the Akademe was far from a parochial institution.

There are three men, in addition to Jones, whose connec-

tions with the organization deserve particular mention. The
first of these is Alexander Wilder, who served as editor of
the *Journal of the American Akademe* for its first four volumes. He was one of the enthusiastic organizers of the
Akademe. Although his visits to Jacksonville were not regular he still exerted a wide influence on the group and he was
a particularly close friend of Jones. So was Block. These
men were often engaged in long controversies over Platonic
themes, so long in fact that they would often forget mundane
interests such as food. Mrs. Jones would come in and say in
her unobtrusive but pointed way, "Come, it is time for ter-
restrial refreshments" or, "We must have some every-day
ventilation in here." Wilder wrote a number of papers for
the Akademe on such subjects as "The Soul," "Life Eternal," "Philosophy and Ethics of the Zoroasters" [Zoro-
astrians], "Ancient Symbolism," and "Creation and Evolution." These titles hardly indicate the range of his thought,
for he was well up on the whole history of Platonism and
had a store of knowledge of oriental thought as well, perhaps best demonstrated by his contribution to *The Platonist*. Block, earlier referred to in connection with the Plato
Club, was influential and in more regular attendance, but
his written contributions were not as numerous. His paper
on "Platonism, and Its Relations to Modern Thought" [22]
was particularly important. He was also a poet and in addition to contributing many poems for publication in various
journals in the Midwest he had several books of poetry published. His great contribution to the movement lay in the
essentially Platonic tone of his literary works. W. T. Harris
deserves particular mention, not so much for his great influence upon the group as for the importance in thought and

[22] Printed in *Journal of Speculative Philosophy*, XVIII (1884), 33–52.

education which he had in his own right. He contributed
several papers, including those on "Plato's Dialectic and
Doctrine of Ideas," "Aristotle's Doctrine of Reason," "Relation of Homer's Poetry to Plato's Philosophy" and "The
Concrete and the Abstract in their Practical Relations to
Life." The first and last of these indicate something of what
Harris got out of Plato and also something of what he interpreted philosophy to be. In the former he emphasized the
dialectical character of Plato's thought and the archetypal
principles to which it led. The latter indicates his conception
of philosophy as the orderly revelation of absolute truth
through a dialectical procedure; he was apologetic for this
paper, regretting that he had been unable to present a paper
on "a truly philosophical subject." The paper was on the
question of universal liberty and the duties which liberty
imposes, "a truly philosophical subject" from any other
standpoint than that of a convinced Hegelian.

When the American Akademe first started it was hoped
that its proceedings might be published in *The Platonist*,
which had been established by Thomas M. Johnson in 1881
for the furtherance of the study of Platonic and Neo-
Platonic sources. A number of the early papers were published in this journal, but it was suspended temporarily in
the summer of 1884 because of lack of funds. This left the
Akademe with no means of making its papers available to
the nonresident members. The Jacksonville group thereupon
considered the possibility of getting out its own journal, a
plan which was finally consummated in March, 1885, with
the decision to publish ten issues a year, each one covering
the Akademe meeting for that month but also including
miscellaneous contributions by its members. The first volume
started not with the March meeting of 1885 but with the

October meeting of 1884, and the issues of this volume were quickly printed to make possible the start of a second volume in the fall of 1885. *The Platonist* was running again by this time but no attempt was made either to combine the two or to abandon the new journal which had been started on its way. This magazine had the name *Journal of the American Akademe*, and Alexander Wilder was its first editor. From October, 1884, to July, 1888, issues came out regularly, but at the latter time Jones was planning a trip abroad and it was decided to disband the organization and its journal for the year. The Akademe resumed its activities again in the fall of 1889, but the *Journal* was not resumed until the fall of 1890. Two more volumes came out under the editorship of Louise Fuller, but the number of issues was decreased to eight. The Akademe disbanded in June, 1892 and the *Journal* was discontinued at the same time.

Study of the papers and critical comments on the papers as recorded in the *Journal* gives a fair idea of the character of the American Akademe. As stated earlier, it was largely influenced by the Platonism of Jones and others. Jones, who read about one paper per year, ordinarily discoursed on Platonic subjects with such titles as "Man—Spirit, Soul, Body," "The Philosophy of Conscience," "Ideas," and "Man and His Material Body," although on occasion he chose others such as "Philosophy and Its Place in the Higher Education" and "Physical Evolution and the World We Live In," which he approached from the standpoint of his Platonic bias. Papers were read on other philosophic themes with such titles as "The Aristotelian Philosophy and its Influence on Subsequent Thought," "The Nature and Origin of the Causal Judgment," "The Analysis and Differentiation of Energy as the Basis of All Philosophy and Religion," "The

Finite and the Infinite—Time and Eternity," "Thought Movements in Relation to Scientific Investigation," and "The Intellectual Element in Matter." Others were closer to the field of religion than philosophy, indicated by such topics as "Our Need of the Ideal," "Christ and Creeds," and "The Glory of God Revealed in Man," and by papers dealing with such subjects as the Bahai Faith, Zoroastrianism, and Swedenborgianism. There was a Swedenborgian element in the group, to some extent represented by Louise Fuller, although when charged with being a Swedenborgian she denied it. In the last year or two of the meetings there were papers on "The Philosophy of Health" and "Mind-Cure," indicating an element akin to Christian Science. Yet no one religious point of view captured the Akademe. There was an interest in most of the newer points of view in religion without allegiance to any. This is perhaps what Johnson meant when he referred to the "heretical orthodoxy" of the Akademe.

On the whole the religious tendency of the Akademe was liberal for the time. This came out rather clearly when Rev. C. F. Bradley of Quincy presented his paper on "The Growth of Religious Symbolism, or the Origin of Christian Rites and Dogmas" in 1891, in which he argued that the rites of Christianity were in existence before Christianity, that symbols of all kinds are representative of the universal rather than the particular or parochial, that all religions are impermanent and inadequate manifestations of an eternal truth. One minister present opposed the thesis as destructive of the finality of Christianity but Jones summed up the general view as well as his own when he said:

The theorem of the paper, that the Christian religion is not a new religion is high ground, and the research worthy of the most earnest and able investigation. I have always been perplexed with the view that the adequate religious illumination was not achieved until eighteen hundred years ago; that the good Father just then got a new and better provision than the previous ages had accomplished. The truth is, that Christ is God with us, but in this fact there is no ground of inference that God never was with any other people.[23]

Most of the members were quite immune to cults which sought simplified means for solving the essential problems of life. This is well illustrated by the reaction of the members who attended Thomas Davidson's Glenmore Summer School, which was founded in 1890, and at which there was evidently an ample supply of cultic sympathizers as well as a goodly array of philosophic talent in the personalities of Harris, Davidson, John Dewey, Henry Gardiner, and others.

Several members of the Akademe spent part of their vacation at Glenmore and report good lectures, choice spirits, delightful conversation, superior wisdom and a sprinkling of enthusiasts of various cults that gave the spice of variety to the entertainment. Vegetarians, (third syllable long) luxuriated in native fruit and "garden sass." Christian Scientists worked miracles of self-healing and general persuasion, and the *Kneipers* had the sunrise all to themselves for the dewy simplicity of their nature worship. Like the man (outside his wife's reception) who *"didn't like to disturb the ladies at their devotions,"* our members said and did nothing in particular, but enjoyed the generous bill of fare immensely.[24]

The emphasis throughout the history of the Akademe was on "high thought," meaning by that term thoughts having relationship to a realm of eternal forms or ideas, as distinguished from thoughts associated with the commonplace and transitory. There was little question raised about the

[23] *Journal of the American Akademe,* V (1891), 184–85.
[24] *Ibid.,* V (1891), 252.

truth of such ideas as the existence of God and immortality. The idea of God was an essential part of the Platonic philosophy which permeated the atmosphere of the monthly gatherings, although God was called by a variety of names, such as First Cause, Absolute Energy, Absolute Mind, and Perfection. Immortality was an equally accepted belief, based largely on the necessary infinitude of a soul which was only temporarily associated with the body and whose essential nature linked it with the divine. On the membership card presented to all members was a butterfly which was an historic symbol for the soul; the motto, "The Soul; aye, the Immortal," was printed in Greek. There was much discussion on the subject of immortality, indicating that the members were well aware of the contemporaneous attack upon this belief and that they thought rational defense of it to be necessary.

The subject of evolution came into the picture on numerous occasions and created considerable stir. The champion of evolution was Elizur Wolcott; the best summary of his position is found in a paper entitled "The Theory of Evolution," which he presented on May 20, 1884. Wolcott argued that evolution was the greatest idea which the nineteenth century had produced and held that it had grown out of a new empirical attitude. He advocated the thesis that "what is not scientifically known, is not *known*, however it may be believed." [25] He argued that there was an obvious development in external nature and that there was a parallel internal development of the mind, and stated the basic idea of evolution to be the thesis that all things come into being by a natural process which makes them effects of that which precedes. Spencer and Fiske, he thought, were the best ex-

[25] *The Platonist,* II (1884–85), 105.

pression of this point of view, and he held that all scientists and some religionists had already accepted the theory. Science, he felt, had always won its battles with religion and would do so in this case. This necessitated shifting the basis of religion from theological concepts to moral ideas.

This paper was somewhat of a bombshell in an organization whose members had accepted Plato's story of the creation of the universe and his interpretation of the nature of the soul. Jones was as mild as anyone in his criticism, attacking first the empirical approach which Wolcott advocated and second the finality with which Wolcott defended the theory. He suggested a possible compromise by saying that as a phenomenological law it could be true without violating the idea of the creation of the universe by God. The secretary seemed to express the majority viewpoint in writing, "It was decided, however, that the doctrine of evolution could in no wise be embraced, until certain gaps which are still yawning can be bridged over." [26]

Wolcott's essay was undoubtedly the incentive which led Jones to present a paper at the first meeting the following fall (September 15, 1885) on the subject "Physical Evolution and the World We Live In," in which he further developed the suggestion made in his criticism of Wolcott's paper, arguing now that the criticism he had of scientific investigation was that it assumed the veracity of sense-impressions and ignored the problem of explaining how the sensory world came to be what it is. He held that matter is reducible to force and force predicable only of an entity which serves as a substrate from which all material phenomena are evolved, a substrate to be defined as pure Intelligence and omnipotent Will. The paper was not a denial of physical

[26] MS, "Records of the American Akademe," p. 31.

evolution but a criticism of the materialistic interpretation which had been made of it.

This paper was followed by those of others who attempted to find a way of accepting evolution without disturbing either Platonic or Christian ideas, and the method proposed by Jones seems to have been the one most commonly adopted. Rev. A. B. Morey read a paper on February 15, 1887, entitled "Christianity and Evolution" in which he defended evolution but argued for a theistic interpretation of it over against what he called atheistic and agnostic interpretations. More important was Wilder's paper on "Creation and Evolution" presented September 15, 1887. Wilder accepted evolution as descriptive of the development of material entities as they are polarized by energy, but argued that energy is dependent upon an energizing source, which is the Absolute. Emanation of all existences from this Absolute was prior to and causative of evolution. The only real change necessitated by evolution was to conceive of the universe as created by a process which took aeons of time, rather than by an act of immediate creation.

The naturalistic trend of the age, however, did make a dent in the Platonic armor of the Akademe, and more so as time went on. While Wolcott fought the battle almost single-handed at first, others joined him as the meaning and implications of evolution became clear. Charles Caverno of the University of Colorado read a paper in February, 1892, on "The Intellectual Element in Matter," in which he took a vitalistic position, arguing that matter is possessed of intelligence, that matter and mind were inseparable and that the natural order is self-contained. He was of course attacked by some members of the Akademe for making no provision for the supernatural and for not attaching due importance to mind. Even in 1892, however, there was still a strong antimaterialistic sentiment, as is evidenced by Wolcott's defense of Caverno. Wolcott said:

I will ask leave of the American Akademe upon the rehabilitation of matter inaugurated here by this paper. It has been the practice of the Akademe to depreciate matter—treat it as rubbish to be swept out. But you know the adage: "You may drive out nature with a pitchfork, but it will come back." Traduce, attempt to degrade or ignore matter as you may, here it is all the same, all the time your best friend, closer than a brother—warming, clothing, nourishing you three times every day, furnishing heart and brains with vital forces—lifting you up to claim kindred with the gods, even when you have just vilified it as *"brute* matter," *"dead* matter," etc. You have shown less respect for matter than the Brahmin does. . . .[27]

The Akademe and the Plato Club were not much interested in philosophical research for its own sake. The historical interest characteristic of the St. Louis Movement and of Thomas M. Johnson was not strong in Jacksonville. Instead, emphasis was placed upon creative thought, a type of creative thought which led to the solution of essentially human problems and gave those solutions metaphysical undergirding. These people were not amateur scholars, they were amateur philosophers with a body of thought which they found congenial as a guide but whose facets were sufficiently numerous to provide a wide diversity of opinion within the framework of its universally accepted categories. To speak of the movement as an amateur one is not to discredit it, for at times it rose to heights of professional proficiency. It was an amateur movement in the sense that none of these people gave their complete time to philosophy and

[27] *Journal of the American Akademe,* VI (1892), 147.

none of them wished to become so involved in technical issues as to disqualify themselves from participation in the solution of immediate and personal problems. It was professional in the sense that one figure, Jones, became a professor of philosophy and gave systematic form to his thought. Jones was the center of the whole movement. Without him the movement would have lacked direction; through him it achieved unity and power of expression. It is important, therefore, to acquire a coherent picture of Jones' philosophy in order to understand the impelling force which kept the movement alive and active. To such a presentation we shall now turn.

CHAPTER III

THE METAPHYSICAL GIANT

No living man provided Jones with the content of his thought. A number, however, did provide him either with inspiration or with insights which he could fuse with his own interpretive analyses.

First, in point of time, was Emerson. The Concord sage has often been referred to as America's most typical philosopher. Whether or not this judgment is merited, it is a commonplace that he influenced more young men in the middle of the nineteenth century than any other American figure. Hiram K. Jones was one of these. Had Emerson not inspired him as an undergraduate, Jones might never have found in Plato the source of his philosophy and thus might never have become known as the outstanding exponent of Platonism in this country. How thorough Emerson's own study of Plato was is open to question but he was at least enthusiastic over Plato and transferred this enthusiasm to Jones.

A second early inspiration was Alcott, despite the fact that the better Jones knew him, the less highly he regarded him. When they first met in Jacksonville and talked philosophy in the 1860s, Jones was just beginning to study philosophy while Alcott was a mature, if not a systematic, thinker.

Jones immediately became attached to him. Jones' visit to Concord in 1878 and his subsequent lecturing at the first four sessions of the Concord School brought their friendship to a peak. By the end of this time, however, Jones had rounded out his own point of view to the extent that Alcott's oracular philosophizing had lost its early appeal and knowledge of Alcott's life was sufficient to convince him that Alcott was no example to follow. When Jones taught at Illinois College after 1886, he referred to Alcott as a type of thinker a college student should try not to be. Yet Alcott's early influence must not be overlooked. He met Jones when Jones needed counsel and, being a master of advising others despite ineptitude in controlling his own affairs, he was impressive. He encouraged and inspired Jones, and gave strength to this prairie doctor who was wholeheartedly plunging into the study of philosophy.

Others, directly and indirectly, had their effect upon Jones. Tayler Lewis, Thomas Taylor, J. J. Garth Wilkinson, Alexander Wilder, William Torrey Harris, S. H. Emery, Jr., Denton J. Snider, and Thomas M. Johnson all were influential to greater or lesser degree. Among his personal acquaintances no one attracted Jones more than Wilder. They met in Concord in 1881, were constantly together at the sessions in 1882, and were partners in the founding of the American Akademe in 1883. Wilder visited Jones on numerous occasions, the last in 1897, when he spent several months in a futile attempt to help Jones prepare his lectures for publication.

Jones, however, can hardly be explained by reference to his acquaintances, literary or personal. They were important, but like the Plato Club, more important for their comments and criticisms, their suggestions and stimulations, than for the actual ideas which they imparted to him. Jones was independent. He had a technique of study, a form of discourse, and an effervescence which were distinctly his own. His thought was not merely rewritten Plato, transmitted to him by his elders or contemporaries; it was a philosophy hammered out through years of study, discussion, and writing, and tempered by the daily round of a physician who met people at their best and at their worst. Jones was challenged by the indecision of the times; he was haunted by a desire to solve the problems which were raised, nourished in this quest by the most inspiring philosopher of the ages, and driven by a passion to make his refuge the refuge of all. Jones' achievement was the achievement of a man who sensed the insecurity of a changing world, found a salvation suited to the vagaries of the day and hour, and strove to give that salvation meaning for others. Regardless of whatever judgment one might have of Jones' philosophy today, its contribution at the time was in providing a way of understanding which raised life to a transcendent unity above the stream of chaotic daily events. More than that, Jones was instrumental in reviving the Platonic philosophy and in making it serve useful purposes in the growing maturity of the midwestern mind.

Jones' thinking went through three distinct, yet overlapping, stages. These are to be designated less by dates than by the psychological imperatives involved. They may be called the oracular or prophetic, the evangelical, and the systematic. The first period, the oracular, was characteristic not only of Jones but of many others at the time. It was a period when men like Emerson and Alcott, along with their transcendental colleagues, gave voice to the growing independence and self-consciousness of America. The political revolution had long since passed. The problems of settlement and national security appeared to be well on the way to solution. The American mind was turning rapidly from the external perception of problems to the internal evaluation of their meaning. It was becoming conscious of itself, of the gains which had been made, and of the open future. This shift from adjustment to a world of physical and social events to expression of internal thoughts and feelings was not only an American tendency. It was found on the Continent and in England in the romantic reaction to eighteenth-century empirical and atomistic thought. Yet, to a considerable extent, its strength was greater in America because of the fertility of an independent intellectual soil and a freedom from historical precedent. Its exponents were no more outspoken than those in Europe but there was clarity and even license in American transcendentalism which defied the canons of traditional discourse. It was natural for this expressive sentiment to be oracular rather than rational, for it was developed in the absence of any particular restrictive phase of culture. Alcott was most characteristic of this temper of mind, the other transcendentalists exhibited it to a lesser extent. As Alcott, Emerson, and the Concord group served to express New England self-consciousness, so Jones, although younger, served a similar purpose in the Midwest.

What has been referred to as an oracular period of thought both in American culture and in the life of Jones had some points in common with Scotch metaphysical writings but otherwise was quite unlike the philosophies characteristic of the Age of Reason. Its spokesmen were annoyed by attachment to the world of sense and obsessed by the lure of the world of ideas. Their technique of discovery was not logical consistency but conscious recognition. They regarded the deeper feelings of men as more important than their rational conceptions. They believed in an intuitive power of the mind, or soul, higher than the intellect or understanding, whose focus of attention was not the world of physical events but a world of spiritual reality. Enamored of such a view, these men could hardly be expected to exercise great restraint in making judgments. The wonder is that anything but intellectual anarchy resulted. Yet the facts show quite the contrary. The movement had internal consistency despite its prophetic quality. This was as true of Jones' early period as it was of other thinkers. An air of finality and revelation did not diminish the homogeneity of the ideas involved.

The oracular period of Jones' thought was at its peak during the early years of the Plato Club in Jacksonville. In the sessions of the Plato Club Jones had opportunity to give free reign to the random movements of his mind. He wrote in his notes (no date): "The genius of the Platonic method is its aim that you shall think rather than remember Plato's or anybody else's thoughts." This is symptomatic of the use to which he put Plato. He mastered the text, to be sure, but he obviously regarded it less as a body of truth to be accepted than as a symbol of truth to be sought. As far as the members of the Plato Club were concerned, they seemed just as anxious to glean wisdom from Jones as to know what Plato said. This is evidenced by the notes taken by members of the club. Jones produced in his analyses what amounted to a commentary on the dialogues of Plato, rich in imaginative and spiritual imagery but meager in content, as far as textual criticism is concerned.

Before starting to read the *Republic* in 1873 he said to the group:

When the spirit has laid up treasures which will not corrupt, then it is rich. We must desire increments of growth to the spirit each day, as the body must take up homogeneous increments in order to support it.

True riches is the receptivity of divine things, a certain activity of the soul toward divine things.

The love of gold, not gold itself, is an evil thing. So the love of divine things, not our stock of them,—that is the good. . . .

We want to read the idioms of various faiths, to become enlarged.

The subject of the Republic is the regenerate life, the progress of the natural to the spiritual.[1]

This is indicative of the perspective in which Jones viewed Plato. The ancient sage was a means of evoking the inspired thought of his readers. Thus, with equal force, Jones could speak in his interpretations on the relation of the sexes, the meaning of science, the value of social responsibility, or the security of solitude, whether or not Plato had touched on these themes. Jones' flow of speech was indefatigable and his range of ideas unlimited. Plato was the source, but Jones was the activating genius.

In this period Jones' dependence was upon intuitive insight, and he defended this source of knowledge even in his later systematic period. He spoke with certainty undimmed by recognition of logical difficulties and his followers accepted his interpretation of Plato and his own insights with equal conviction. The Plato Club was a means of expressing the innermost reflections of his mind; for the members it was a short cut to a realm of unified truth which brought into harmony its plural expression in daily existence.

Characteristic of this period are Jones' notebooks, somewhat difficult to catalog because of the lack of dates and the

[1] MS, Notes of Mrs. Sarah Denman, I, 29.

intermittent use to which he seems to have put them. Since Jones was a physician by profession these notebooks were not limited to philosophical reflections. On one page would be a list of patients, on another an expense account, and in the remainder were interpersed prescriptions, medical analyses, and bits of philosophical wisdom. Jones might well have written a philosophy of medicine, for he included many explanatory notes on such subjects as the nervous system and cholera, but he evidently was little interested in organizing them. A few samples of his more philosophical notes are the following:

Man in nature is the perpetual problem—the Sphinx's Riddle.

The appetites and passions subordinated are useful servants but they make very bad masters. They should be as trained hounds, obedient to the mandate of the reason and judgment. Health is this reasonable and just control.

Man derives his wisdom from God and his love mediately from woman while woman derives her love from God and her wisdom mediately from man.

A prime element in philosophy is the clear discernment of the correlatedness of cause and effect, that throughout the realms of nature and of mind they are correlated in discrete and not in continuous degrees. So that in all things cause is utterly exempted of its effects and this is most plainly maintained and manifested between the realms of matter and of mind. Mind is eminent and native in the prerogative of causation and matter distinguished only in the subordination of effects. The law therefore of mind is liberty and the law of matter is fate, or necessity.

In spreading philosophical wings Jones was interested in personal improvement and development. He felt the need of incubation for his own ideas and he recognized the same need in his philosophically-minded friends. A motto seems to have played a fairly significant part in his life at the time, probably one which he composed himself.

Get knowledge from every sort of man
Learn from the booby what you can
Gather knowledge from every source
Knowledge stored is vital force.

This expresses something of the raw practicality of the western mind. There was a spirit of dauntless courage in the thinking of these people. Few were the inhibitions to restrain their mental gyrations and slight was the modesty in giving them expression. Jones took a fling at poetry, hardly comparable to the work of Louis J. Block, but expressive both of the undisciplined sincerity and the naïveté of a mind raised above the concerns of material existence, yet drawing upon the figures of speech characteristic of an agricultural world. His poem, "Growth," is worth viewing in this perspective.

'Twas a little seed in the dark cold ground
That said, "Why must I slumber here
With the mists and dampness all around,
Where no ray of light can ever appear?"
    And a voice shot down on a beam of the sun
    One morning before its birth was begun
    And said, "Little germ, why murmur you so;
    It is your business to lie there and grow."

A soul within a body chained
Dropped down to earth, despised, reviled,
With darkness and with mists enchained,
Unconscious of the life that smiled.
It said, "Why am I prisoner here?
Why chained in form of clay so low?"
    And a voice dropped down like an angel's tear
    "Be quiet, soul; 'tis your time to grow."
And thus every darkened place of earth
Holds some secret germ of a brighter day,

And where there seems to be mold and dearth
There shall the richest glories play.
And for every struggling soul that sings
And murmurs in its march so low
There shall bud and blossom an angel's wings

. . . . .

So comfort, dear hearts, and use time to grow.

In this period of Jones' thoughts the birth of ideas was primary. He grew increasingly convinced of the creative power of the mind. As Plato had often resorted to the use of allegory and myth, so Jones came to view all thought in a somewhat similar vein. Thought was the human way of expressing truth, but truth was not always perceived in the same fashion. This should not be taken to mean either that Jones regarded truth as plural or all opinion as equally valid. For him, as for any Platonist, there was a difference between opinion and knowledge. Knowledge was the correct perception of truth and was largely attainable. Language used in expressing truth was symbolic and it was thus language that was allegorical.

Alcott was somewhat impressed by Jones when he first visited Jacksonville, but according to the judgment he made of him after their January, 1871, meeting he was not as convinced of Jones' philosophical ability as he was eight years later when the Concord School began. It is interesting to note that Alcott at the time made the same criticism of Jones that Jones later made of him. After this early meeting Alcott said:

He shows a subtle sense of the force of thought itself along with a massive symbolism which has the effect almost of poetry on the imagination, giving a mystic tinge to his utterances. His method is analogical, mythical, mostly, I might add, allegorical.

He applies his method as well to Swedenborg, Goethe, Shakespeare, as to Plato and his school. . . . With a fancy liberated
from his understanding he was a poet and pure idealist. . . . I
do not yet find that he commands my full faith in his method or
ideas, but I might however in the presence of a mind unique
and powerful and prompting to a fuller acquaintance. . . . It
were connert to see what impression he would make on our Boston Radical Club. Most likely as the great obscurist and enigma-
tist.[2]

As Jones continued his study of Plato, the outline of a system gradually took form. Plato was a guide and not only
stimulated the thought process but also afforded a sense of
direction for that process. In the first period of Jones'
thought, Plato was a means; in the second period, the evangelical, Plato's thought, or better yet, the truth to which
Plato's thought referred, was an end. Jones moved from the
emancipated expression of ideas as ideas to the free development of ideas as truth. The first period was not only a
conditioning of Jones' mind; it was also a convincing of his
mind. The true, the real, existence, substance, essence—these
had become important and Plato provided the deepest insights into their meaning. The early period's slow solidify-
ing of conviction led to the next one, a period of propagation of the Platonic gospel which had come to be accepted in
its broad outlines.

Plato came more and more to be a symbol for philosophical reflection and Platonism the name for a spirit of thought.
Jones increasingly transferred his allegiance (although this
process was never complete) from the study of Plato with a
small group to the propagation of "Philosophy" to a larger
circle, although the Plato Club was Jones' first public audience and its members were willing recipients for his own

[2] MS, "Western Evenings: An Itinerary," 1870–71, p. 143.

thought as it took form. He came to view the club as too provincial for the furtherance of a universal system of thought, and he therefore sought a wider sphere for his message. The first phase of this evangelical program was limited in geographical extent. Outside of Jacksonville he visited Quincy to give spirited impulse to the group there and spoke intermittently before the Plato clubs in Decatur and Bloomington which had been established by Mrs. Julia Palmer Stevens, one of his most devoted followers. He hoped to establish clubs wherever a significant interest in philosophical speculation was in evidence. This intention was made clear in a letter to Thomas M. Johnson on December 5, 1875:

Platonism is a silent but irrepressible force. It proceeds philosophically. Its voice is not heard from pulpit or rostrum but it proceeds from the other end of the line, establishing itself in many independent ideal social centers, which are gradually being multiplied in the process of the social development. It is destined to become one of the major forces in the ultimate social determinations of the country.

The program moved slowly. Outside of the groups relatively close to Jacksonville the only circle worthy of mention was that started by Johnson in Osceola, Missouri. This, however, was not of long duration and was relatively ineffectual, as were those in Decatur and Bloomington, because of a dearth of philosophical talent. It is little wonder, then, that Jones viewed the founding of the Concord School of Philosophy in 1879 as a real opportunity for the furtherance of Platonism among representatives of a more cosmopolitan public. The idea was not originally Jones', but his visit to Concord for conversations in the summer of 1878 finally brought the idea to fruition. Jones became one of the two main lecturers for the first four years, William Torrey

Harris, the other. He was happy over the prospects of the Concord School. After the first session he wrote Johnson that it had established the fact that there was great aptitude and taste in America for philosophical reflection. He wrote in the *Jacksonville Journal* that the aim of the Concord School was "to establish the first principle of the universe as a conscious personality." What he expected of the school is not difficult to see; he viewed it as a real chance for propagating his favorite gospel.

Jones was opportunistic in regard to the Concord School, but he was more than that. He went on to supply what they wanted, for he was already regarded as the leading Platonist in the country and everyone knew what to expect from him. James McCosh spoke highly of Jones in his report of the Concord School.[3] Alcott regarded Jones and Harris as the real strength of the program. He wrote (July 23, 1881):

Mr. Harris and Dr. Jones, this session as during the former, are favorite teachers, and draw the larger classes. They bring their authorities in thought and methods from the past schools of philosophy—the Greek and German—and are themselves masters of their themes. This wins the attention and confidence of their hearers, and this is fortunate for the reputation of the school.[4]

Newspaper accounts and other records of the school all seem to agree on the esteem in which Jones was held. He represented the spirit of the school better than anyone else, including Harris. One editorial writer said, in speaking of the trend at Concord:

They have grasped the great principles which underlie the world-wide side of religion, and have been able to translate them into

---

[3] *Princeton Review,* IX (1881), 57–58.
[4] Odell Shepard (ed.), *The Journals of Bronson Alcott* (Boston, Little Brown, 1938), p. 525.

the life of our own time with such modifications as the time demands. Particularly has this been the case with the lectures of Dr. Jones. The strength of his utterances has been a growing surprise to those who have listened to him. They have enunciated at every point the superiority of force to matter, the correspondence of energy in nature with the intelligent forces which are above nature, and the immortality and eternity of the soul as the great fact in which centres all that makes life worth living. These truths have been enunciated with Plato always in the background, but again and again have they been held up to view until their importance could not but be felt and acknowledged.[5]

The summer before the Concord School opened Dr. Jones and others from the Midwest had been invited to Concord where Dr. Jones displayed his talents before a small but select group including Emerson, Sanborn, Channing, and others of philosophical ability and prestige. Alcott's estimate of Jones by this time was very favorable. He was enthusiastic about Jones' capacity; after a week of discussion he said: "A more profound student of the Greek school of philosophy we probably have not in any part of the country. . . . Without him our age would lack its complemental mind, idealism its truest interpreter." [6]

Jones had the allegiance of the Concord sages after 1878. His pilgrimage East on this occasion was but a prelude to a greater opportunity during the next four summers when he lectured before a large clientele at the Concord School. He promulgated Platonism, lecturing solely on Platonic themes. He made an attempt at synthesis in these lectures but the attempt fell short of what he accomplished in his later lectures to the students at Illinois College. The titles he chose for the Concord lectures during the first three years varied

[5] MS, Scrapbook of Mrs. Hiram K. Jones. The name of the paper is not known.
[6] *Ibid.*

somewhat from year to year, but the content was much the same. Representative were the titles of the 1880 lectures. They were: "Cosmologic and Theologic Outlines," "Platonic Psychology," "The Two Worlds and the Twofold Consciousness," "The Eternity of the Soul and its Preexistence," "The Immortality of the Soul and the Mortality of the Soul," "The Psychic Body and the Material Body of Man," "The Education and Discipline of Man," "The Philosophy of Law," "The Philosophy of Prayer," and "Spiritualism, Ancient and Modern."

In 1882 he entitled the series "Christian Philosophy" but the essential spirit of the lectures was far more Platonic than Christian, except as one may desire to equate the two, and the content was similar to the lectures of the previous year. To conceive of these Concord lectures as expressive of Jones' final thought would be unfair, since the Illinois College lectures are more developed and orderly; it is worthwhile at this point, however, to single out one lecture as an example of the system-making that was already under way. These lectures were the beginning of a system which had elements in common with Plato and the Neoplatonists but was unique in its own way. The lecture, "The Immortality of the Soul and the Mortality of the Soul," in the 1880 series, is symtomatic. Here he argued (having in previous lectures held that the soul had existence independent of the body) that the eternity and immortality of the soul are not the same; the first, he said, has to do with the actuality of the soul's existence, the second with the quality of its existence. He then went on to distinguish three aspects of the soul, resident in the cranium, thorax, and abdomen respectively; they were denominated the intellectual, volitional, and sensuous. Each had an object peculiar to itself; for the intellectual it was love of truth, for the volitional the love of honor, and for the sensuous the love of riches. Immortality, the qualitative existence of the soul, was achieved by virtue of the first controlling the other two aspects. The soul was essentially an emanation from the creative force of reality (Plotinus). The further from that force the soul migrated, the less immortality it had. He distinguished personality from individuality. Personality was the essence of the soul, individuality an attribute of personality. On this basis he contended that there are many individualities which can express our personalities and that these individualities all have counterparts in nature. This led him to conclude that the lower orders of nature developed from man, rather than the reverse.[7] Man's moral responsibility, he argued, was to control the lower orders of nature both within and without.

This summary, however brief, indicates that Jones was developing a philosophy with some unique elements, not only in terminology but also in content. The increasing systematization of his thought did not diminish his missionary zeal, however. If anything, it only added to it. Concord gave him an audience which was both receptive and relatively large, and the attention given him added to his confidence.

Jones left Concord after the 1882 session, not to return again. He was evidently aggrieved that the other leaders of the school refused to move it west. There is no doubt but that a large following went east to Concord, and Jones felt it only fair that the West should be given a chance to show what it could do. Alcott, in particular, was stubborn, and the school remained in Concord. Jones, by this time quite confident that the West could develop its own philosophical

---

[7] He later modified this judgment.

center, broke away from the school, and in the fall of 1883 the American Akademe came into being in Jacksonville. This was not to be a reading club for the study of Plato; it was to be a center and medium for the expression of philosophical ideas for the whole continent, centrally located as it was. Jones' emphasis upon the Platonic canon declined somewhat with this new plan, but his desire to propagate "Philosophy" was as strong as ever. When it became clear that attendance at meetings was to be principally local, a journal was started to provide for the absentee members, for it was thought that *The Platonist* was hardly adequate to meet the needs of the Akademe. *The Platonist* had been in existence since February, 1880. Jones wanted the various independent philosophical movements throughout the country to fuse their forces in one organization. When *The Platonist* was having financial difficulties in 1884, Jones suggested the magazine be turned over to the Akademe with Johnson to be retained as editor but with the name changed to *Philosophy*, to preclude any charge of provincialism. Johnson declined the offer but this situation does establish the relatively broad motive Jones had in founding the Akademe.

Additional evidence of Jones' crusading zeal is to be found in his correspondence with Johnson at this time. On August 27, 1883 (when the plans for the Akademe were being made) he wrote: "We must organize all the available material from Maine to Texas—and as soon as may be, as soon as some considerable number of apple carts have accumulated, we shall call a meeting and vote them in." Again on September 26, 1883, he wrote: "I find everyone pleased, to whom I have presented the *causi* and *modus operandi* of our project. . . . I meet in all a genuine enthusiasm and hearty support. . . .

A continental commonwealth of 400 persons, the cream of our country, so aggregated, organized and interested, will give our cause a continental victory."

The story of the Akademe need not be retold here.[8] Suffice it to say that Jones secured his four hundred members (nominally at least) and the membership was not only continental but international in scope. While the membership was not entirely "the cream of our country," it did include people of prominence, some of whom possessed real philosophical ability. Despite Jones' professed cosmopolitanism in philosophy, Platonism, at least idealism, did dominate the organization. Jones so defined philosophy that certain types of philosophy were necessarily excluded or put at a disadvantage. A characteristic definition, which he used for many years as the first sentence of his first lecture to Illinois College students, was this: "Philosophy is the pursuit of the knowledge of Being as Being, in its essence, and in its cause and causation, and in its effects." The positivist, among others, would hardly have found an intellectual atmosphere such as this particularly congenial. The result was that few who were not idealistically inclined associated themselves with the organization. It was, nevertheless, a rather remarkable organization for its day, preceding, as it did, all the professional philosophical associations by nearly twenty years.

In 1886, Jones was asked to lecture to Illinois College students, an opportunity which he immediately accepted. The Plato Club, the Concord School, and the American Akademe were all adult education programs; here was a chance for Jones to instruct a different age group and he

[8] Refer to pp. 52 ff.

seized the opportunity. This was in line with his desire to make Jacksonville a real teaching center. He said (in miscellaneous notes, written sometime during the 1880s):

Cities and communities like individuals are subject to the law of division of labor. One town must be agricultural, another commercial, another mechanical, another political, another educational. The last is the highest. I am proud to call ours the Athens of the West and shall do what I can to make her so. Teaching, the growth of mind, be our forte.

The first year he gave only fifteen lectures to the senior class. Then he extended his course until it took permanent curricular form. Jones was successful in his college teaching (he continued until his health began to fail in 1900; he was then eighty-two). Fifty years later some of Jones' students could repeat sentences and paragraphs from his lectures verbatim. He was popular with the students, and they dedicated the college annual (The Rig Veda) of 1897 to him. How fully they understood what he had to say is difficult to ascertain; that they went away with some knowledge of philosophy, as viewed by a Platonist, is certain. One great value to Jones in this experience was that he was forced to systematize his thought more than ever before. He never liked to write. It is doubtful if he ever wrote all of his Concord lectures, although some of them are in manuscript form. But the undergraduate mind was more exacting than some of his listeners at the Plato Club or at Concord, and a course of lectures which had to be delivered throughout the year, rather than at a summer school of a few weeks where he delivered ten lectures at most, demanded more elaborate treatment. Thus was inaugurated, or rather continued—since it had already begun at Concord—a third period of his intellectual life, that of systematic statement of his philosophy.

Jones was a tireless worker. Considering the fact that teaching was but a sideline and that he had one of the best medical practices in the city, bringing him an income of from $6,000 to $10,000 a year, it is a tribute to his vitality, as well as to his thoroughness, that he not only wrote out all of his college lectures but continuously revised them. Two complete sets of lectures have survived in manuscript form along with miscellaneous annotations and sections which he had revised. The first of these two sets had no title but was divided into chapters with marginal headings. The second set was entitled "Outlines of Philosophy" and is in the handwriting of Alexander Wilder, who helped Jones prepare it for publication. That it was never published is due more to Jones' disinclination to polish his work than to its inferiority. He was disturbed by the inadequate treatment his Concord lectures received in the newspapers, and he talked about preparing them for publication, although his intimates knew this would probably never be done. A few of his articles were printed in the *Journal of Speculative Philosophy, The Platonist,* the *Bibliotheca Platonica* and the *Journal of the American Akademe,* but the bulk of his work was never ready for the printer's ink, at least from his standpoint. He projected a number of books during his career but none saw the light of day. One was "The Elementary Philosophy," another, "Elements and Outlines of Philosophical Speculation," and a third, "Plato in America"; it is conceivable that the first two were merely substitute titles for what finally did mature in "Outlines of Philosophy." In any event, he wanted to have "Outlines of Philosophy" published.

In 1897, he was hard at work improving its style. To be certain it was in good form, he invited Alexander Wilder to spend several months helping him improve his style. Mrs. Julia Palmer Stevens summarized this situation as follows:

About five years ago Dr. Jones had Dr. Wilder there for a few months trying to straighten out the manuscript which he found very difficult. He said (privately) that when he put the sentences into good grammar, that Dr. Jones said he had changed the meaning of them. He said Dr. Jones used so many unnecessary, emphatic terms and repetitions. But Dr. Jones told me that "Dr. Wilder took all the gist out of the subject," and so he did not do the work. The same objection was made to Mr. Block, on trial.[9]

After the failure of these attempts to improve his manuscript with the aid of Wilder and Block, Jones did little with it. His health was not good, and old age weakened him, although he continued his medical practice. After his death, all of Jones' writings were left with Miss Clara Calvert, a relative who had kept house for Jones from the time his wife had died in 1891. It was thought she might get them in shape for publication, as she was capable of doing so. Mrs. Stevens also considered attempting the job, for she had been as close to Dr. Jones through the years as almost anyone, but this never materialized. Finally the manuscripts were sent to Johnson in Osceola, but poor health prevented him from giving them attention. The result was that Jones' mature philosophy never reached the larger public he had always hoped to influence. For the statement of his philosophy we shall rely largely on the last series of lectures in his own handwriting for it is significant that he returned to these in 1898, after using Wilder's revision in 1897; they

9 Letter to T. M. Johnson, October 10, 1904.

would seem therefore to be the preferred statement of his position. To distinguish these from "Outlines of Philosophy," we shall refer to them as "Lectures." Before turning directly to these, however, it is well to speak briefly of Jones' Platonic studies.

Jones was more the Platonic philosopher than the Platonic scholar. At the same time he was familiar with almost every detail of Plato's writings and knew the major scholarly interpretations of them. His one real claim to distinction as far as contributions to Platonic scholarship are concerned was his judgment that the *Laws* was a Greek satire on the Platonic system and hence not Plato's writing at all. In writing to Johnson (April 12, 1876) he expressed the view that this was a really new idea and asked Johnson, who was fast becoming a capable Platonic scholar, what he thought of the idea. There is no record of Johnson's reply, but the letter makes clear that Jones felt he had discovered at least one thing other scholars had overlooked. His judgment that the *Laws* was spurious was not new, for German scholars such as Suckow, Strumpell, and Ribbing had so declared it years earlier, but his interpretation of it as satire does have some claim to priority. Other than this, Jones made no real contribution to Platonic scholarship, though his allegorical interpretation of the dialogues was somewhat distinctive. The Plato Club was largely a religious circle for the glorification of Plato. Jones and the other members of the club were more interested in the overtones of the dialogues than in the order of their composition, differences in literary style, and the like. Jones' allegorical method made possible numerous deductions which were meaningful to the club members, if not always academically defensible; examples are plentiful in the notes taken by club members.

Outside of these notes, only two interpretations of the dialogues are now available but these two, one on the *Symposium* and the other on the *Republic*, provide some idea of the flavor of his Platonic studies. Let us turn first to the *Symposium*. Symbolically, for Jones, this dialogue represented the "banquet of life." The house of Agathon, where the event took place, signified the "house of the good;" Socrates represented philosophic wisdom; Aristodemus, public virtue; Agathon, the good heart; Aristophanes, civic conformity; Eryximachus, health; Pausanias, temperance; Phaedrus, love of beauty; Apollodorus, divine inspiration; Glaucon, celestial light; Alcibiades, exaltation of life; and Diotima, religious cognition. Jones regarded Plato as a teacher, one who used his dramatis personae to serve intellectual and moral ends. He saw in the dialogue not the record of a night's revelry but the symbolization of fellowship turning its attention to philosophical, scientific, and moral problems. He said, "It is unmistakable that the theme of this drama is not wine but love as a dominant factor in the nature and history of existence." [10] The outcome of the whole dialogue, according to Jones, was that love was regarded not as emerging from the physical but rather from the spiritual, from the soul in its union with Being.

Jones' interpretation of the *Republic* was published in the *Bibliotheca Platonica*.[11] Here he argued that there had been much misunderstanding of the *Republic*, that many had been led to believe it was a seriously presented social polity. He argued that as a philosopher Plato's concern was with first principles, which meant that the actual constitution of a state was quite secondary in his mind to a consideration

[10] MS, "The Banquet."
[11] "Key to the Republic of Plato," I (1890), 255–73.

of the principles upon which a state might be justly founded. He thus contended that the principle of justice, not the form it took in institutions, was the theme of the dialogue. He held that the realization of justice in any state was but "a feeble and inadequate transcript and pattern of the Idea of Justice." [12] Justice, therefore, was a logical cause and actually transcendent of its effects upon particular social organisms. As such, it was not an objective phenomenon even though its effects could be observed: "Justice itself is subjective, ideal, essential, causal, celestial in God, and psychic in man; while its political existence is phenomenal." [13] The *Republic* was a "soul polity" rather than a social polity; its object was to chart a path of existence for the soul so that it could distinguish between the transitory and the permanent and, having done so, direct its attention to the achievement of that harmony of self which was alone productive of phenomenal justice and righteousness.[14] Jones argued that Plato used language symbolically, that the biography and history included were but a form of myth, an imaginative way of approaching the meaning of justice. Plato's real object, hence, was to challenge the reader to improve his own soul and work for its salvation through self-perfection. This could be achieved only by vigorously seeking truth concerning the ultimate causes of things upon which knowledge of justice and its subsequent achievement in action were based. This way of interpreting Plato suggests why Jones rejected the *Laws* as spurious, for if Plato were engaged in searching for first principles alone he would most likely not have given specific form to them as statutes. At the same time it would have been pos-

---

[12] *Ibid.*, p. 258. [13] *Ibid.*, pp. 259–60.
[14] This provides the setting for the remarks at the opening of the study of the *Republic* at the Plato Club quoted earlier. See p. 73 above.

sible, although more difficult, for Jones to have interpreted the *Laws* allegorically too.

Jones argued that in the *Republic* Plato conceived of the absolute goodness and truth of God and the eternality and immortality of the soul as the principles upon which every worthy motive and action rested. Wisdom, honor, honesty, knowledge, health—all the virtues were dependent upon them. He held that Plato conceived of the soul as a microcosm with a capacity for comprehending the macrocosm and its principles. Education consisted in bringing into consciousness the potential knowledge which the soul possessed. When awakened, the soul, gifted with a limitless source of harmony, could reduce the varying potentialities of life to order through knowledge of how true order, or justice, was to be achieved. This, he argued, was the motive of the *Republic,* dissociated from the purely political interpretation which some had placed upon it.

It should be apparent by now that Jones regarded the dialogues more as allegory than as statement of fact, metaphysical or otherwise. With this interpretation, one can understand why he spent less time in minute analysis of the dialogues than in contemplation of the sweeping visions which they afforded. These visions provided him with a superstructure for his own philosophical system, the details of which he could fill in by the scintillations of his own mind. To this system we shall now turn.

Jones regarded philosophy as the knowledge of Being as it is in itself, as it is in its causes, and as it is in its effects. Philosophy was therefore to be distinguished because of its supernatural, rather than natural, content and meaning. It was concerned with the primary reason for things, not the phenomenal existence of them; these two were to be clearly distinguished because phenomena could not possess their own *raison d'être;* an object and its cause were two separate entities. The focus of attention was essentially the world of nonphysical causes.

Philosophy defined in these terms, according to Jones, grew out of an essential need of mankind, a need for unity of knowledge and for an understanding of events. Man was forever in search of knowledge of God and of the nature and destiny of the human soul. Even in childhood he was accustomed to ask questions about the why and wherefore, and this quest was an essentially natural one which continued through life. Jones held as an axiom the principle that man could acquire knowledge of whatever he was conscious. It necessarily followed that since man was conscious of a causal order and the existence of his own soul he could know and understand these individually and interrelatedly.

Jones conceived philosophy to have three functions, critical, logical, and moral in nature. Philosophy as criticism, because of its broad vision, provided orientation for the more particularized studies of man and served as a check on the temptation to view these special studies as of universal importance. He was more critical of the physical scientist than of others, but this is easily understood since physical science at the time was rapidly extending its boundaries and freely asserting its claims to finality. Jones regarded Darwin as an example of the type of one-sided personality which too arduous concentration upon science developed. His criticisms of Darwin were two, defended by reference to Darwin's own writings: he had lost sensibility for the nonphysical elements in culture such as religion and art; he had failed to care for the elemental physical needs of his own body. Jones felt that the job of the philosopher was to apprise

the scientist of his partial insight and of the relative position
of his special field in the whole organon of knowledge. He
was just as critical of the religionist; as an example of an
extremist here he referred to Alcott, whom he characterized
as a man who had failed to develop an ability to exercise
judgment in the ordinary, everyday problems of human life;
he cited the Fruitlands experiment as representative of Alcott's impracticality. Philosophy as criticism could see
things in perspective and could challenge the claims of the
partisan who sought too great finality within one field of
interest without consideration of the relationship of that
particular field to others.[15] Philosophy was concerned with
language too, with the selection of terminology appropriate
to the subject and with the relationship of words in descriptive and explanatory discourse, a concern which was both
critical and logical in import.

The logical function of philosophy was to seek harmo-
nious relationship among the various bodies of knowledge,
to see them in their causal connections and in their appropriate stations in the hierarchy of truth. For Jones this was
the heart of philosophy, associated with its critical function
to be sure, but aiming at a codification of truth which explained the phenomenal world and gave knowledge of its
causes. This logical, or metaphysical, or speculative, function was more or less a technical one, one which demanded
training and discipline, but one which provided society with

---

[15] "The man devoted and absorbed exclusively in spiritual and religious interests is not whole; he is not sound; he is not healthy; he is
diseased spiritually and physically. And the man who is devoted and
absorbed in physical science as an interest exclusively is equally not
whole, not healthy, unsound, diseased physically and spiritually." Lectures. III, 30. (Page numbers on I and II are continuous, but with III
the numbering starts with page 26. This is due to revision of the first
two sections without renumbering of the pages.)

the meat which philosophy alone could supply. In demanding specialization, Jones argued philosophy was similar to other fields. He said:

But so, also, the many are not mathematicians, or boot-makers, or blacksmiths, or carpenters, or rulers, or teachers, or artists; but in order that each shall realize the highest well-being, he should derive from the service of all the others, boots from the bootmaker, and clothes from the tailor, and dwelling from the carpenter, and merchandise from the merchant, and grain from the farmer, and bread from the baker, and civil order from the ruler, and education from the teacher, and physics from the scientist, and metaphysics from the philosopher; and the wise use of all these contributions from all these servants, together with his own performance, is the practical wisdom of the denizen of this planet.[16]

This leads us to the third function which Jones conceived philosophy to have, the improvement of the moral fibre of mankind. This was neither to be achieved by a Sunday-school catalog of virtues nor by courses in ethics to be taught in colleges or elsewhere, but by giving direction to human action through knowledge of the nature of reality and man's relationship to it. An adequate metaphysics, therefore, would provide an acceptable ethics. If men knew the true value of the soul as distinguished from the body, realized the worth of the nonphysical against the relative unimportance of the material, there need be no worry about morality. The knowledge of truth, in true Socratic optimism, would lead to action in accordance with it. As the converse, he argued:

Persons who pursue show and trumpery rather than ideas, who appreciate simulation and display more highly than the essential

[16] *Ibid.*, I, 19.

and the real, who seek after the delights of the body rather than the wisdom and beauty of the soul—these must fail of the true delight and the golden treasure of philosophical acquirement.[17]

There was little time spent on the subject of practical ethics in Jones' lectures. He did speak commendingly of the balanced life, of the value of good health, of work, and of a broad curriculum during the period of training, but he spent the major part of the time on metaphysical subjects, depending on the properly exercised intuitive sense to provide sufficient knowledge in the moral realm. He defended the breadth of the liberal arts curriculum, for he regarded inclusiveness of knowledge as the best preparation possible for living. As a curricular study, Jones conceived philosophy to be liberating. He defended it because it sought knowledge of first causes and provided perspective and moral incentive, but he also regarded it as excellent training of the mind for independent thought. He said:

But what is chief as an end, and more than all this can be, is the philosophic mental discipline and habit and power of true thought, which cannot consist of accumulations of other people's opinions of whatever sort, true or false. The ages of thought are perpetually renewed by fresh draughts from the original fountains; and not by means of accumulations of ancestral gymnastics. We may, and should, acquaint ourselves well with their performances, but we must also acquit ourselves in the performance. The manna must be gathered fresh every morning. The art of philosophizing is something else and more than literary intimacy with philosophical systems.[18]

A statement as strong as this (and there are others equally forceful) would seem to indicate a fairly "progressive" teaching technique. This seems difficult to square, how-

[17] *Ibid.*, I, 20.   [18] *Ibid.*, II, 35–36.

ever, with the doctrinaire spirit he is reported to have exercised and the clear delineation of a system which his class lectures contain. Perhaps he thought the best way to get students to think was to tell them what to think—or perhaps he thought that the presentation of a unified system would give the student more to wrestle with than would a bird's eye view of many different systems. His technique, however good or bad it may be judged, was commonly practiced in the colleges at the time.

Jones conceived of philosophy as primarily concerned with three bodies of truth: physics, metaphysics, and theology. Logically conceived, they ran from theology to metaphysics to physics, but psychologically apprehended, the order was the reverse. Physics dealt with the phenomenal world (nonbeing), metaphysics with the realm of mind (being), and theology with vital forms (spirit, or life). Man, existing largely in the second of these three worlds, stood midway between physical nature and deity. Since man held this intermediate position, it was necessary to begin philosophical investigation with consideration of the nature, form, and limits of knowledge, and thus more clearly to distinguish the types of knowledge he did possess.

All knowledge, for Jones, began with the act of consciousness. For him, there could be no knowledge of things of which we were not conscious; whatever we were conscious of was potentially knowable. He divided consciousness into three types: that of the sense mind, of the psychic mind, and of the pneumatic mind. There were three basic forms of knowledge: sensation, scientific perception and philosophic apperception.[19] The realms with which these dealt were in

[19] This should not be taken to mean that each of the three forms of consciousness was limited to a single appropriate form of knowledge.

turn those of apparition, nonbeing (in itself), and being (in itself). Other terms he used for these realms were appearance, phenomenon, and idea. Jones held that we ordinarily start with sensation. Sensation was limited to immediate recognition of external objects, not in their true phenomenal existence but in their unreliable appearances. To explain the difference between the forms of knowledge, he used the example of a house. A picture of it made by a painter was its appearance, the structure reared by the artisan was its phenomenal existence (nonbeing, by definition), while its true form was its existence in the mind of the designing artist (being). This analogy was not exact; at least it did not adequately represent the interpretation Jones made of appearance elsewhere. Appearance was not alone a secondary reproduction of an object; it was, in fact, primarily the object as known through sensory observation.

According to Jones, sensory observation, although first in order, was not to be accepted as final since it was inaccurate and misleading. He spoke of it as a "camera in which the apparitions of phenomena are inverted and reversed from the true order of the phenomena." [20] He hardly meant this to be taken literally; all he seemed to mean was that sensation proper was not trustworthy and that higher forms of knowledge were needed to check it. But these higher forms of knowledge had their appropriate types of sentience. Physical contact was characteristic of sensation proper, and it was this and this alone that Jones was questioning. The psychic and pneumatic minds had sentient principles of

---

In philosophical investigation, the sense mind was limited to the realm of physics, the psychic mind could rise no higher than metaphysics, but the pneumatic mind was inclusive of all since it dealt with the primary causal principle.

[20] *Ibid.*, III, 40.

their own seated in man's inner nature and these were important for higher forms of cognition. He said: "He [man] must feel and perceive in order to be conscious in and to know throughout each of the departments of knowledge." [21] Just as empirical knowledge was rooted in the physical sensorium, so scientific and philosophical knowledge were grounded in sensibilities characteristic of their types. The importance of these inner sensibilities can hardly be overemphasized, for Jones made much of them, although Scotch metaphysics seemed to have little appeal for him.

Scientific perception, said Jones, was corrective of the misapprehensions of sensation. The function of science was to distinguish between physical objects as they appeared to be and as they were. It was largely classificatory and descriptive, but to a degree was explanatory, as well. By means of demonstration and inductive inference it provided physical explanations for natural phenomena. Its main task, however, was to provide perceptual knowledge of phenomena as they really were. But in this task it was always hampered, because it was forced to deal with effigies, or images, rather than with reality itself. Hence a third form of knowledge was necessary: philosophic apperception.

The great difference between these two forms was that scientific knowledge was forced to deal at second hand with reality while philosophic knowledge was direct. "The pure intellect looks at the essential form, not its effigy. This is an at-looking and an at-beholding, and so is apperceiving, a taking hold by the mind of the form itself, in mental immediacy with it." [22] Proof in this realm was the evidence of immediacy. The pneumatic mind, and to an extent the psychic mind, had an innate capacity to achieve this level

[21] Ibid., III, 42 b.   [22] Ibid., II, 42 d, e.

of knowledge. Scientific knowledge was partial; philosophic knowledge was complete. Scientific knowledge was fragmentary; philosophic knowledge was unified. Scientific knowledge was limited to phenomena; philosophic knowledge was capable of knowing ultimate causes and essential being.

Philosophical knowledge was the culmination of the whole process of knowing. It checked the inferior forms and provided them with basic principles. It brought harmony into the realm of truth. "And this insight of the pure intellect in this apperceptive relation to truth, superadds the other links in the chain of knowing, and comprehends and consummates the whole truth, viz., the truth of appearance, and the truth of phenomenon, and the truth of the essential form of being." [23]

Truth, to Jones, was not plural, but singular. There were, of course, many truths, but they were all a part of one essential truth. The whole was not to be found on any one level of knowledge but rather through the assimilation and coordination of all three levels and by means of the superior unifying powers of the psychic and pneumatic minds. The sense mind worked a posteriori, the psychic mind, a posteriori and a priori, and the pneumatic mind, a priori alone. What was dim or beclouded on the lower levels was clarified and harmonized on the higher plane. Through philosophy alone knowledge of the immutable and causal could be achieved; sensation and scientific perception were but means to that end. Dialectic was the technique by which the correlation of knowledge took place. Philosophic knowledge was contemplative; it began with the a priori concepts supplied it by the sentient principle of the pneumatic mind and became expanded into a totality by logical deduction.

[23] *Ibid.,* III, 42 ff.

After dealing with the power to achieve and the nature of knowledge, Jones turned his attention to the nature of mind and matter and their relationships. He posited the existence of an Uncaused Cause, based upon the pneumatic sense and attested to by men throughout history. He also posited as created substances mind and matter, a universal duality, the first a creative, active, intelligent force and the second a receptive, passive, unintelligent instrument. He made three basic distinctions between them. Mind was the knower and matter the known, mind the cause and matter the caused, mind the form and matter the formed.

For defense of the first of these distinctions he referred to the three forms of consciousness which were possessed by mind and never by matter. Thought was not an activity of the brain; it was a quality of the mind which used the brain as a tool. Matter was observable and observed but never did the observing.

The second distinction Jones regarded as requiring more proof, and this he dealt with at some length. The ideas of cause and effect, he held, separated philosophy from science. Science was largely descriptive whereas philosophy was basically explanatory; science therefore dealt largely with effects and philosophy with causes. He held that philosophy alone was finally competent to deal with efficient causes, thus preempting for philosophy what is now generally regarded as a function of the special sciences as well. He regarded the relationship between cause and effect as "the golden chain that binds in unity all the multiplicities of the system. And it is the key to the secret of the relation of essence and phenomenon." [24]

There were three basic principles governing cause and

24 *Ibid.,* IV, 53.

effect: (a) cause and effect are correlates; (b) they are discrete in their relations (an important principle for the development of his system); and (c) cause is logically prior to its correlated effect. The mind could not only identify these, but also know them in their correlatedness and separateness. But Jones was not satisfied that even this armory of presuppositions was sufficient to make clear the distinction of mind as cause and matter as caused. He thus added five other axioms which not only served as a basis for what followed but also summarized the tenor of his argument. They were as follows:

1. That the material principle and the life principle are two distinct principles, as the universal active and passive; and that in their relations to each other they are discrete,—the one cannot by any continuity or change become to be the other nor the other the one.

2. That the distinctive characteristic and property of the life principle is force, intelligence, self-motion, energy [intelligence is hardly interchangeable with the others]; and that the distinctive characteristic of the material principle is inertia, rest.

3. The cause of motion is force; and the life-form is forceful, and so self-moved.

4. That which is self-moved may be a cause of motion in other things.

5. That which is not self-moved cannot be a cause of motion in other things. Wherefore the material principle, itself void of motion, cannot cause motion in other things.[25]

On the basis of these axioms Jones described matter as unable to change itself, demanding motion from outside, and also as void of feeling, willing, thinking, and determining. It was therefore Nonbeing since it possessed none of the attributes of Being. It could best be spoken of negatively,

25 *Ibid.*, IV, 59.

as "something which is lifeless, senseless, motionless, form-less, and void and empty of all absolute or positive quality and property." [26] Matter was inert, and as such possessed no essential qualities or powers except that of being ener-gized from without. All nature, organic as well as inorganic, was matter provided with power of mobility from outside. What seemed to be qualities of matter, such as quantity, size, and weight, were accidents of matter, effects of motion upon it. By so limiting matter, Jones could speak of it as that which is caused and refer to mind (often spoken of as the life principle), which possessed by definition powers of self-motion, and the like, as that which causes.

He was emphatic in stating that matter was devoid of essential properties. The taking on of organic form did not change its basic nature. Neither could the discoveries of physical science invalidate this conclusion. "Neither mag-netism, nor electricity, nor other is endowed with life or thought or feeling or self-motion any more than the stone or the clod or the grass of the field." [27] Matter was merely the instrument by which mind achieved its purposes. He con-sidered it absurd to conceive of it as possessing any of the qualities given to mind.

Now matter, in order to be perfectly subordinate and subservient and instrumental to mind, must have no life of its own, no force of its own, no will, no thought, no end, no aim of its own else it would be constantly disappointing you, so that when you have spent time and labor in making your house, or your ship, or your garment, tomorrow the material may have walked off and left you, or it may have dissolved into other forms and uses.[28]

In spite of the fact that Jones made matter little more than dependent potentiality, he still conceived it to be important.

[26] *Ibid.*, IV, 60.   [27] *Ibid.*, IV, 67.   [28] *Ibid.*, IV, 67; V, 68.

It was necessarily existent as a complement of mind, as an instrument. A cause had to have its effect, and without matter mind could not realize its desires and ends.

Man was the microcosm, and his existence was representative of the whole of nature. To understand the relationship of man and his material body would clarify the distinctions between mind and matter, causally and through form, in all nature. Jones defined man as a being, self-moving, feeling, thinking and knowing, capable of developing the arts and sciences and various forms of human institutions. These qualities which man possessed were the qualities of mind, not matter; hence man was essentially a nonphysical being. True, he argued, the mind and body are linked together, but they are correlated while retaining their discreteness. The essential nature of man was spiritual (mental), not physical. The body was not basic because it was but an instrument which the mind used. It did not control man; neither did it, nor could it, exercise joint control along with the mind; it was subsidiary and derived its form as well as its motion (action) from the mind. The third distinction, therefore, between mind and body was that mind provided form and body assimilated it.

Mind (or soul) was the cause of form, since form could inhere only in that which was self-moved. The body, as instrument, could partake of it but could not create it, do away with it or even modify it.[29] The true nature of man was revealed in his thought, his speech, his knowledge, his scientific work, and his artistic and social institutions. These were not functions of the body nor were they dependent upon it. What made them possible was a "psychic" existence

[29] "Be it propounded here that the material body of a man is no more a constituent part of the man than is the engine a constituent part of the engineer." *Ibid.*, VI, 91.

which was independent of the body in essence, though associated with it in existence; the fact that these contributions could survive an individual, a social group or a race was evidence of their nonphysical origin. Uncertain of the logical compulsion of his own case on this point, he invoked the authority of Plato, Paul, and the Pentateuch, all freely interpreted to serve his purposes. He also argued that the mind was the cause of form because the body, being subject to the law of change, could not explain continuity within a life cycle; only the existence of an abiding, form-controlling element separate from the body could do so.

A further argument Jones had for the mind's power of design was based on his belief that the mind could experience and know independently of the physical senses. Affections and thoughts were nonphysical in nature and existed prior to any expression through the material body. Man could think of a complete act, such as lifting a book, without making one physical move toward that end. He could experience love or hate, or know them to exist either in his own life or in the lives of others, without physical perception. The list of things the mind could know nonsensuously was long and impressive and by no means limited to love and hate, as the following makes clear.

And so also of justice and of injustice, of truth and of falsehood, of right and of wrong, of liberty and of slavery, of beauty and of ugliness, of ambition and humility, of virtue and vice, of morality and immorality, of reverence and insolence, of obedience and transgression, and pride and vanity, of life and death and immortality and freedom and God, and the soul itself and the souls of all living creatures, of all living forms of the essential and immaterial worlds, all the physically invisible natures, it knows without the use of the material organs.[30]

[30] *Ibid.*, VI, 108.

Since mind was able to experience ideas and forms independently, it also had power to cause these forms to take on physical properties. By virtue of this, mind served not only as a causative principle but as a designing one as well.

With mind established as different in essence and function from body, it was easy for Jones to conceive of them as separable. It was on this basis that he defended the immortality of the soul (or mind, since he used these terms interchangeably). The soul was an everlasting entity which inhabited the body for a period of time; the body was merely a temporary vehicle. Death was the departure of the soul from the body, and the body thereafter slowly disintegrated. To be consistent, Jones should have argued that the soul departed slowly from the body in order to explain the process of bodily disintegration, but he thought it sufficient merely to state that the soul separated itself from the body, causing death.

The distinctions between mind and body in man were equally applicable to the difference between mind and matter in the universe at large. There were two distinct substances, one a thinking, causing, designing substance, the other an unthinking, uncausing, and undesigning one. He called these "essential," or "vital," existence and material existence. The realm of essential existence consisted not only of the mind but of all other forms which the mind could know. Jones argued that since all objects had characteristics in common with their own type, horses, lions, or men, archetypes were necessarily presupposed. Hence a world of forms, or ideas, subsisted in the realm of entities, real beings; these were active, causative, creative, formative, and made possible their physical effigies; they were permanent, their representations, temporary.

These forms, however, were more than models; they were a self-active source of all the motion and organization in matter. Their orbit moved from their perfection in being to their imperfection in Nonbeing; if it were not for their existence and particularly for the vitality characteristic of that existence, neither motion nor form would be possible in the physical world. Both nature and art were alike in this respect. In regard to the latter, Jones held that neither the mechanical nor fine arts could be understood except through the essential forms from which all art emerged. He gave as an example the Eads Bridge at St. Louis, characteristic as it was of the Midwest during this period. The true bridge, according to Jones, was not the bridge of its physical parts but the idea-bridge, a form-bridge, in the mind of Eads, for, he argued, if the physical bridge were to be destroyed it would take more than the parts to reconstruct it; it would take the ingenuity of Eads, whose mind originally conceived it. This bridge, as all mechanical achievement, was but the fruition in material form, not only of ideas possessed by the architect or inventor, but of ideas whose archetypes were in the world of entities. This he held was true of all mechanical devices "from a steam engine to a hoe handle." The fine arts were equally impossible without perfect forms of which artistic creations were symbolic and representative. The forms, and themes, of art were permanent; these were resident in the invisible world of entity from which art in every period of history derived its existence. In the divine mind existed ideas of beauty, love, justice, freedom, etc., and flowing from these perfect forms were the lesser forms which in turn created the shape and organization of phenomenal objects. The psychic consciousness apprised man of the forms which existed as mental ideas and concepts; the pneumatic consciousness gave him knowledge of the higher order of forms which existed in the mind of God.

Physical nature was just as much a product of the world of essential forms as were the arts. Jones argued that a true cause had to be sufficient to explain the existence of its effect. To have a true science of nature, it was necessary to have a science of essential forms, or divine forms. The form of an object was its true reality.

Form as thus distinguished from bodily manifestation is therefore the essential, determinate reason and nature of every living creature. And each of all the corporeal aspects of animated nature depends from its own peculiar, differentiated and distinguished *essential vital form*. Indeed there is not anything in all the kingdoms of nature, animal, vegetable, and mineral that is not what it is by reason of its essential forms.[31]

According to Jones, there were two substances: material substance, which was receptive of form, and essential substance, which provided form and vitality to matter. To truly read the book of nature, the vital element in matter had to be traced to its source, the life-principle in form. Jones said, "All *protoplasm* is *bio*plasm," and by this he meant that every object in nature was infused with a vital force, a force which emerged from the world of forms.

As form was characteristic of entity, as against material existence, so also was intelligence. Certainly, he argued, there could be no order and no intelligence in that which was formless, lifeless, almost qualityless. Form was predicated of nonmaterial Being alone. Wherever form was, there order was also, for what was form if not the placing of qualities in orderly arrangement? Order, or organization, demanded intelligence, both in terms of its creation and in terms of the

[31] *Ibid.*, VIII, 131.

end for which it was created. If matter, inert and formless, ruled, there could be nothing but chaos. On the other hand, intelligent entity could provide organization for the smallest material object as well as for the whole. Jones held that a teleological power worked through nature providing it with direction as well as motion and form. This gave his system the character of an immaterial determinism. He thought, however, that he escaped deterministic implications by distinguishing between an outer and an inner aspect of things. The outer was the phenomenal show, the inner the form and energy supplied by the life principle. Real determinism, most idealists of the period argued, was found only when the phenomenal was said to be ruled by the phenomenal; Jones, along with others, seemed to feel that what was ruled by something beyond or above escaped this noose.

Jones rejected the doctrine (as distinguished from the law) of organic evolution on the basis that it assumed material existence to possess energy, form, and direction in itself. Organism, from his point of view, could not result from a purely material process; it was essentially the result of the activity of vital forms working on plastic matter. He distinguished being from existence. The former was the life process, the form itself; the latter was the cycle through which the life process vitalized matter and returned to itself. The doctrine of organic evolution was concerned with existence but since it violated the life cycle characteristic of existence it could not be true.

Existence, as Jones conceived it, consisted in an orderly process, a rotary motion about an axis. The line of the motion was that of a gyre, a spiral motion proceeding from center to circumference and return, with the center itself always in motion; its course was, therefore, the advancing or "perpetual" circle. Jones regarded this as the course of unmodified motion, characteristically found in the atom, the cell, the monad, and the movements of the stellar bodies. It was also found in modified form in the other orders of life. The original nature (created) and the cycle of life constituted an object's form and the embracing of matter by it provided existence for a living organism. Organism was hence the effect of form upon matter.

The higher up the ladder of material nature, the more numerous and complex cycles of energy were found to be. Man was the most complex order of all. Some of the same cyclical processes found in lower orders were characteristic of his existence, examples being the circulation of the blood and the organization of the nervous system. Yet man had numerous cycles which were peculiar to his level. To understand his material existence one had to know the numerous and varied vital motions governing it. The important point to remember is that Jones conceived the existence of all material orders to be dependent upon their respective cycles of energy and not upon properties inherent in matter. Differences were explained by the various life motions characteristic of each species or class.

And there can be no other reason for the differences, and the everlasting perpetuity of these differences, between the material bodies of the monad, and the mollusk, and the dog, and the eagle, and the horse, and the man than that the inside of the organism, the invisible life motions in their circuits differ by so much. And these invisible motive systems are the different forms, and they are different by original creation. And in the material sphere they clothe themselves in fitting costume. Nobody ever did see, or ever will see, one of these creatures clothing himself with the costume, the bodily shape and guise of some other form of life. There is no such thing as the crossing of these lines of species.[32]

32 *Ibid.*, VIII, 144.

While Jones closed the door on the total Darwinian hypothesis, he did acknowledge the power of a given species to develop within its own cycle. The fact that he viewed the cycle as spiral rather than circular is evidence of this.

The center and circumference in living forms advance so that the circuit does not meet the center at the same point where it left it on setting out. Hence progress is a great word and now and then becomes popular. It is true not in the sense of one growing out of his own nature and type, but progress in the measures and moments and ends in one's own nature, within the soul, rather than in circumstantial relations.[33]

How form, or vital motion, could evolve in itself and yet not produce something more in the process Jones never explained. To evolve means to develop new qualities of some kind to greater or less degree. Development within a species demands explanation in itself, and viewed from our standpoint today it is certainly a vital step on the road to acceptance of evolvement from one species into another over a long period of time. Jones accepted the fact of evolution, but not in terms of its theoretical statement at the time, nor in terms of the physical explanation given it.

The tendency to interpret phenomena in terms of physical law was growing during Jones' lifetime. He was fearful of the effect which this tendency might have and hence turned to an analysis of the nature of law, physical and otherwise. He studied Spencer's materialistic explanation of nature and gave considerable time in his lectures to a presentation and criticism of Spencer's point of view, at the same time defending an idealistic interpretation of law as preferable. Law to him was the order given to phenomena by mind. " 'Law' is but the observed order and force of an intending personal mind and will." [34] He argued that physical scientists

[33] *Ibid.,* VIII, 146–47.   [34] *Ibid.,* X, 183.

(he quoted Faraday) were explaining matter in terms of force, thus admitting that matter was incapable of effecting either action or form of itself. All evidence pointed to the conclusion that the laws of matter were provided from without and that they were but an expression of higher laws. This was as true of social laws as it was of physical laws.

The laws of man arise not nor subsist in the physical environment of his life, but in his intellectual and ethical constitution and social nature. And so may it be affirmed that the laws of God arise not nor subsist in the system of nature, but that the observed order of nature's processes called "laws of nature" are nothing else than the outward manifestations of the intending purpose and will of a supreme being.[35]

Physical science was, of course, valuable. As a description of phenomena it was important but it, as well as the phenomena it attempted to describe, had to be seen in the perspective of first principles. There could be no adequate physics without metaphysics, just as there could be no adequate metaphysics without physics. Both were parts of a single process of knowledge.

This duality, the mind and will of the creator and the forms and laws of the created, must therefore be comprehended from the grounds of their differentiation and unity. Either as an abstraction from the other is an untruth in the mind and thought of man. God separated and apart from the world, or the world separated and apart from God,—either alone is not, and never was, and therefore is truly unthinkable logically, except as that which is not and cannot be, a mere concept without a content.[36]

Jones started with the assumption of an Uncaused Cause and two substances, material and essential. When he came to present his thought on the Uncaused Cause, he spoke of it

[35] *Ibid.*, XI, 192.   [36] *Ibid.*, XI, 196.

as a third substance, spiritual by name. It is well to see how Jones conceived this spiritual substance to be knowable.

For each of the three forms of consciousness (sensible, psychic, and pneumatic) the procedure was the same: first, awareness through sensation, then, analysis and synthesis through thought. This was as true, for Jones, of knowledge pertaining to the spiritual world as of knowledge relating to the physical and psychical worlds. The certainty achievable in each was also the same. The pneumatic consciousness therefore had a sense of its own (he denominated this conscience, although intuition might have been a more inclusive and hence a more appropriate term). This sense (conscience) provided man with an awareness of a Creative First Cause; this awareness consisted of a "flowing in" of knowledge, although the use of this language is again somewhat misleading, for what Jones really defended was innate knowledge, knowledge which was ineffaceably in the mind, education and experience serving but to draw it out and refine it. Knowledge of deity was therefore clear, direct, and certain. It was attested to by all individuals, great and obscure alike, and by all races and nations in history. That God existed was as definitely known as that an external physical world existed. Testimony of this was to be found in the realm of morality. In ethics the "inflowing and informing spirit" provided knowledge of right and wrong and of justice and injustice, clearly and decisively. Here the use of the word "conscience" was quite appropriate. Jones argued that it was not man's experience, his training, or his environment that gave him a standard of judgment, but rather the knowledge which came directly from God. The laws of ethics were definite and consistent, based finally upon an understanding of reality as reality.

And just as the mathematical science is the standard of all rightness in physics and mechanics, so is the science of all rightness in the conduct of life established in this consciousness of the "influence" of the spirit and nature of deity. Moral rightness has no other source and subsistence than in the divine nature.[37]

This was, of course, but another way of saying that as man knew God and God's will he knew how to act, still another way of saying what was said earlier, that for Jones knowledge of metaphysics opened the door for knowledge of ethics. What was needed, as Jones saw it, was not a program of morals but an awakening of the moral sense.

Additional testimony for direct consciousness of deity was to be found in history. Jones argued that all great historic movements had their genesis in what he called "religious faith," by which he meant direct consciousness of a Creative First Cause. He held to a theocratic interpretation of history. He argued that no major change, no great development in history, would ever have occurred had it not been for the prior vividness of the knowledge of the nature and will of deity in the mind of man. He said:

Upon careful investigation it will be found to be universal in human history that the social genesis, the origin and movement of all social institutions and social order, proceeds from a consciousness of deity, and that in all the upward and forward movements of human society, the primary and dominant force has been some declared form of religious conviction in which is implicit a system of religious faith and worship and that in this system of religious faith and worship is unfolded a peculiar and distinctive type of civil society with its institutions of civil and religious order, with the government and laws, and education and enlightenment, and public morality and virtue and justice.[38]

As a philosophy of history this sounds obscure from a twentieth-century viewpoint. Jones, however, was not trying

[37] Ibid., IX, 159.   [38] Ibid., IX, 162.

to develop a philosophy of history; he was trying to establish the necessity for consciousness of God by reference to its persistence in history.

Knowledge of God was provided by the pneumatic consciousness directly; knowledge about God proceeded by analysis through logical thought and argument. Jones attributed two major attributes to God, creative power and intelligence. The former was the explanation for the energy and motion characteristic of all spheres of being and the latter for the form and order in existence. The attribute of intelligence has already been referred to; a word or two should be added about creative power. Jones conceived of God as full of energy, bubbling over with vitality and power; it was this quality which made possible all the change, motion, and action characteristic not only of biological phenomena (his own field of specialization) but also of purely physical phenomena. He did not doubt the fact of motion or change, but he wanted to give that fact a setting in metaphysics and theology which the scientists were loathe to do. His handling of the problem of causation on somewhat Platonic grounds with an additional emphasis upon energy makes appropriate the designation of his system as vitalistic idealism. He made room in his philosophy for an active element which more formalistic procedure had discounted and of which his Platonic ancestry had failed to take adequate account.

Jones often drew upon analogies between man and God to clarify his point of view. As said before, man as the microcosm was reality writ small. Deity, Jones said, corresponded to man building himself a home and farm in a wilderness. Such a habitation showed signs of life and form as long as man was there, but upon his departure it lost its energizing force and in time became desolate. Just so, argued Jones, is the universe held together by the energy and thought of the creative process, and were this power to remove itself, the universe would crumble to ashes.

The pneumatic consciousness of God was a certainty, since it was not the testimony of the few but of all men everywhere. The common man could testify as to the existence of God as well as could the philosopher. Where the latter served a special function was in providing content to this universal consciousness. The saint and sage, the prophet and philosopher, all enlarged our understanding of the nature of God. Their investigations and insights were just as important in metaphysics as those of the specialist in science. There were two great priesthoods, scientific and philosophic. Both were benefactors of mankind, and their light enriched the pilgrimage of life.

Exclusive preoccupation in one field, Jones regarded as the cardinal sin of the day. The scientist was likely to assume the self-sufficiency of his own techniques and data. So were others in different fields of interest. Specialization was valid and necessary, but it was rewarding only when the specialist perceived the relationship of his own studies to other bodies of knowledge. Jones believed in the usefulness of science as descriptive; he believed in the necessity of philosophy as explanatory. He spoke as if they dealt with two different worlds, the natural and supernatural, the sensible and supersensible, the physical and nonphysical, but he conceived them to be correlative, not disjunctive. This thought was expressed on numerous occasions but at no time more cogently than in the following paragraph.

And accordingly all human history with the sciences and arts and religions and philosophies of human society comprehends in its genesis the service of both these functionaries, namely, the abstract realistic, or natural science, mind and the idealistic mind. And the world's thought and the world's work and the world's social fabrication could not be got done with either of these forces alone without the other; and if we would know either and justify either, we must know and justify them both at once, as they are coordinated and correlated in their practical unity in the social consciousness.[39]

Jones' idealism was not a reduction of the physical to the nonphysical in Berkeleian fashion. It was far truer to the Platonic pattern, particularly that of the *Timaeus*, than many other idealistic systems. It lacked finality and precision, however, for even in his most systematic work, his lectures to the students at Illinois College, there is a great deal of repetition and certain issues need clarification. The repetition is explainable, perhaps even forgivable, on the basis that these were college lectures and summarization was necessary. But certain rough spots can hardly be overlooked. At times, Jones spoke of two worlds, a physical and nonphysical; at other times he dealt with sensible, psychical, and pneumatic worlds. One is undoubtedly meant to be a classification according to substance, the other according to knowing mechanism, but this distinction is nowhere clear. Then, again, the order of causation is puzzling. In one place he speaks of the first cause as life, the second as energy, the third as vital motions, the fourth as form, and the fifth as organization; in most places, life, energy and vital motions seem to be used interchangeably as do form and organization. These problems and others of less significance should not be allowed, however, to mar judgment on Jones as a philosopher of importance. He was indeed America's outstanding Platonic philosopher, teacher, and protagonist of his day, little known by the present generation because of

[39] *Ibid.*, XII, 222.

the inaccessibility of his works. His importance grows when he is viewed in terms of the prairie country where he largely labored and yet the national, even international, audience which he sought and for a considerable period of time, had.

CHAPTER IV

A PHILOSOPHIC OUTPOST

As has been pointed out, St. Louis and Jacksonville were the chief centers of philosophic discourse in the Midwest. They were rivals in the sense that one was largely devoted to Hegel while the other had its primary affection for Plato, yet co-ordinate in the sense that the philosophies concerned were not in opposition to one another. Each in its own way sought a spiritual interpretation of life, against the growing materialism of the day, each offered a personal orientation for its devotees, and each provided a unifying quality of existence to soften the cruel blows of a disinterested and mechanical universe. The Hegelian and Platonic groups were not limited in their influence to the members and visitors who assembled in St. Louis and Jacksonville, nor to the more cosmopolitan audience which listened to their separate claims at Concord. Both possessed a missionary zeal enlivened by the persuasiveness of their leaders and both served a missionary purpose by carrying the gospels of Hegel and Plato into territory ripe for some integrating way of life which placed institutional and personal problems in perspective.

The St. Louis group had influence in such places as Terre Haute, Indiana, where the leaders of the normal school developed a philosophy of education along Hegelian lines. The Jacksonville group spread to Decatur, Bloomington, and Quincy, Illinois, where smaller but nevertheless enthusiastic bodies assembled to study Plato and assimilate the inspirational overtones as well as the positive content of the Platonic system. Among these cities, Quincy was the most active and most productive.

The early history of Quincy paralleled that of Jacksonville although its institutional life was less highly developed and its industrial life more so, making for a larger population. Quincy was named (1825) for John Quincy Adams who was then President of the United States. The first newspaper was established in the early 1830s and was a daily by the 1850s. A Quincy Historical Club was founded in 1840, to preserve the record of the early years of the colony. A town library was started in 1841, which served not only as a repository but also as an instrument of adult education through its lecture series, which brought to Quincy national figures who spoke on scientific and philosophical topics. A competitive lecture series sponsored by the Encore Club appeared in the 1850s. From the beginning Quincy had a strong interest in education. Miss Catherine Beecher early established an English and German Seminary which became in succession Johnson College and Chaddock College, the latter offering courses on the college level until about 1900, when it became a boy's preparatory school (Chaddock School). In 1860 St. Francis Solanus College (now Quincy College) was established. In its library was a fine collection of original manuscripts and sources in classical philosophy and literature. The completion of the Galesburg-Quincy section of the Chicago, Burlington, and Quincy Railroad in 1857 gave Quincy direct connection with the East and increased its population as well as aided in its industrial growth. In 1858 one of the famous Lincoln-Douglas debates was held in Washington Park, for Quincy was regarded as an important center in Illinois politics.

Quincy has always had a large German element in its population. Germans began arriving in the early 1830s and this process continued slowly until 1857, after which in increasing numbers immigrants from various sections of Germany, particularly Bavaria, settled there. While this German element should have meant much to the cultural life of the community, particularly as far as philosophical interests are concerned, it is one of the ironies of local history that its greatest influence was upon the commercial life of the city, while Quincy's intellectual life was stimulated and led by more indigenous strains largely traceable to New England ancestry. Quincy's most important amateur philosopher, Samuel H. Emery, Jr., became a Hegelian but there is no basis for assuming that the large German population in Quincy had any influence upon this eventuality.

Nor can it be said that the religious institutions in the community had any appreciable effect upon the direction of philosophical thinking. By 1853, when the population of Quincy was about 10,000, there were over eighteen religious societies, yet the intellectual group in the city was little affected by denominational and doctrinal problems. One of the unique things about Quincy was that even with an oversupply of churches there was little inclination to force allegiance, and the spirit of free inquiry was highly respected. Henry Asbury, one of the early members of the Historical Club and the local historian, said in 1882:

Every year that has passed since I have resided here has weakened the disposition in men to foster the spirit of persecution.

Perhaps we don't believe as much as we used to think we did, yet we feel sure that we are better than we should be if the old time centuries could fasten upon us again their conscientious convictions that we ought to burn some people to save the souls of others.[1]

The two ministers who were affiliated with the philosophical groups in the city, Samuel H. Emery, Sr., Congregationalist, and Frederick L. Hosmer, Unitarian and a noted hymn writer, were of liberal persuasion and offered a stimulating rather than a restraining influence upon the movement. The same was true of C. F. Bradley, a successor of Hosmer, who was an active member of the Jacksonville group.

It is difficult to date Quincy's first interest in philosophical discussion, although it seems to have been around 1865. As was true of Jacksonville, one of the factors which made the movement possible was the New England background of most of the individuals concerned. Samuel H. Emery, Jr. and Mrs. John McFadon were born in Taunton and Edward McClure in Malden, Massachusetts; Mrs. Sarah Denman and James Woodruff in New Haven, C. H. and Lorenzo Bull in Hartford, and Mrs. C. H. Bull in Durham, Connecticut. Others were either born in New England or had returned East for college.

The visits of Emerson and Alcott were an inspirational factor. Emerson lectured in Quincy on several occasions and visited in the Emery home. His effect upon Emery was considerable. They began a long and rewarding friendship when they met in 1866, although Emery had been a fervent reader of Emerson before that date. Emery always thought highly

---

[1] *Reminiscences of Quincy, Illinois, Containing Historical Events, Anecdotes, Matters Concerning Old Settlers and Old Times, etc.* (Quincy, D. Wilcox, 1882), p. 122.

of Emerson. He wrote in 1903, at the time of the Emerson Centenary, "I have often said, and am glad to repeat, that he was the finest gentleman I ever met." [2] Emery likewise cherished the hospitable comment which Emerson made when he moved to Concord (1879). Emerson said, "It was a good compliment to this town, your coming here to live." [3] Emery's contacts with Alcott were equally pleasant, and when he decided to return East to attend law school at Harvard, Alcott invited him to settle in Concord and rented him his own Orchard House. Emery was subsequently made Director of the Concord School, at Alcott's suggestion.

The relations of Emerson and Alcott to Quincy were not limited to their friendship for Emery. Emerson met with private groups for discussion and Alcott stayed for several days at a time conducting "conversations." They were both deeply impressed by the caliber of the minds (largely feminine) with which they came in contact. Miss Harriette Moore of Concord wrote to one of the members of Friends in Council after Emerson had been in Quincy in 1872:

Mr. Emerson told me, after his return, that he had never met with a circle of ladies he so much admired as the circle in Quincy. He said in point of culture and intellect they would compare with any ladies he had ever met. As for Mr. Alcott, he was perfectly carried away with them. You would think, from his enthusiasm, he was in his second childhood.[4]

Alcott constantly referred in his *Journals* to the superior culture and learning of the groups he visited, not only in Quincy, but elsewhere in the Midwest. On December 7, 1872,

[2] Refer to F. B. Sanborn, *Recollections of Seventy Years* (Boston, R. G. Badger, 1909), II, 493.
[3] *Ibid.*, II, 492.
[4] MS, "Friends in Council, Scrapbook with Programs up to 1915–16," p. 31.

he wrote: "For conversing I rather prefer a western company before an eastern. There appears a disposition to deal
with things at first hand, a certain robust handling, rough
perhaps but ready and respectful, that more than compen-
sates for the daintier and more decorous book-training common to eastern people." [5]

The robustness which Alcott attributed to the western
mind fell short of conceit, but it was deeply imbued with confidence and a consciousness of its own importance. On occasion this was embarrassing for the representatives of the
East. After Emerson's 1867 lecture in Quincy, Burrell B.
Taylor, editor of the Quincy *Herald*, wrote an editorial
entitled "Another Bore," quotation from which will indicate
something of the self-confidence and honest discrimination
of the Midwest.

The public had been led to expect much from the lecture of
Mr. Ralph Waldo Emerson, delivered at National Hall, on Tuesday night, to a large and intelligent audience. He had been advertised as "the profoundest thinker in America." It was said
that some British writer—in irony we presume—had so spoken
of him. But like most of these professional lecturers from the
Hub, or thereabout, Mr. Emerson shows that he has read a
great deal more than he has thought. His lecture was literally a
hash from what he had read, and not a production coined from
the mint of the brain. Any man who has read considerably, or
has access to any of the standard Encyclopedias, and possesses
the capacity to write fair English, can get up just as good a lecture as was Mr. Emerson's, and it would not amount to much if
it were not a good deal better. His subject, "the man of the
world," meant anything he might choose to make it, and he made
it mean nothing in particular. . . . We allude to Mr. Emerson's
irreverence for the past, for all things old. It reminded us of what

[5] Odell Shepard, (ed.), *The Journals of Bronson Alcott* (Boston, Little, Brown, 1938), p. 428.

Prentice says: "that Massachusetts has more dead lions and more live jackasses than any other State in the Union; and that the latter are constantly flinging their heels in the air at the former." This is a part of the philosophy of the Hub.

The manner of the lecturer was exceedingly prosy, dull and uninteresting; so much so that quite a number of persons were lulled to sleep by his monotone. Altogether there was a very disappointed, dissatisfied audience, who were more delighted when he finished than when he began. We can hear a much better lecture, any Sunday, in any of the several pulpits in this city.[6]

While people like Emerson and Alcott stimulated people throughout the Midwest on their visits, there were some individuals who had generating power of their own and these were chiefly responsible for the continued interest in philosophical subjects long after one-night lecturers had come and gone. The first of these, as far as Quincy was concerned, was Mrs. Sarah Denman (1808–82), the founder of Friends in Council and benefactor of that organization and other civic enterprises, including the hospital which for many years bore her name. Sarah Atwater was born in New Haven, married Mathew B. Denman in 1826, and lived in Philadelphia until moving to Quincy in 1842. Mr. Denman was a land-agent and a man of means. Mrs. Denman was a feminist and humanitarian. During her life in Quincy there was not a civic enterprise which escaped her attention nor failed to receive her benefactions. Her feminism was not of the crusading variety, yet it was concrete. She initiated the suggestion of holding a women's suffrage convention in Quincy in 1869; the idea was given serious consideration but was never carried out. In 1870, along with other Quincy women, she signed a petition asking Congress for legislation providing for equal rights for women.

[6] The Quincy *Herald,* February 28, 1867.

The establishment of numerous women's clubs in the 1860s was a part of the feminist movement. These clubs served to prepare women more adequately for equal rights and also to provide organizational support for them. Philosophy had its first group appeal in Quincy through a women's club, Friends in Council, which Mrs. Denman founded. It was inaugurated in 1866, although its charter was not granted until 1869. It was one of the first women's clubs in the United States, Sorosis of New York and of Jacksonville probably being the only ones to precede it. It was the first women's club to own a building of its own, a gift from Mrs. Denman in 1878 and still in use on the grounds of The Historical Society of Quincy and Adams County. From Quincy, Friends in Council spread to Lawrence, Kansas; Berlin, Wisconsin; Marquette, Michigan; Burlington and Rutland, Vermont, and elsewhere. As one of the early women's clubs it exercised a remarkable cultural influence upon the maturing feminine mind.

Mrs. Denman's home was where Friends in Council began. She invited twelve Quincy women to gather there on November 16, 1866, to begin reading valuable books together. Through such reading they hoped to fulfill three objectives: (1) to achieve clearer light on the handling of practical problems; (2) to become women of culture through acquaintance with the great works of the ages; and (3) to become better informed about the issues of the day. In the words of Anna B. Bull, they wanted ". . . to cultivate a liberal freshness of thought and feeling though it lead to the sacrifice of many a long and fondly cherished prejudice or theory." [7]

[7] MS, Friends in Council, "Scrapbook with Programs up to 1915–16," p. 93.

Evidence of the feminine independence characteristic of the group is to be found in the names suggested for the organization; they included The Nondescript Club and The Embryonic Free and Independent Anti-Red-Tape Society. Prominent in this early group were Mrs. Denman, Mrs. C. H. Bull, Miss Louise Fuller (who lived in Quincy for a period although her real home was in Jacksonville), Mrs. Lorenzo Bull, and Mrs. James Woodruff. Other early members of interest were Miss Lizzie G. Bull, Mrs. Anna B. McMahan, Mrs. Rose Nelson Clapp, Mrs. John McFadon, Miss Cora A. Benneson, and Mrs. S. H. Emery, Jr. It was decided at the first meeting that the organization would meet once a week and that the first book for reading and study would be Lecky's *The History of the Rise and Influence of Rationalism in Europe.* In sixteen weeks they finished Lecky's two volumes and then turned to Lydia M. Child's *The Progress of Religious Ideas,* which was completed in thirteen more weeks. In regard to this first year of study Mrs. Denman later wrote: "How much information we gained and how much our world enlarged in the course of that travel through the ages, it would be difficult to say. It is well to have the soul widen toward the past, to know the record of our long descent and become conscious of the life that was as well as that which is." [8]

During the second year the group, with an average attendance of from sixteen to eighteen, turned to the reading of the Platonic dialogues. At the end of the year there seemed to be some question as to the advisability of continuing to read Plato because some found him difficult to understand. The next year they started out on Epictetus, but soon re-

[8] *Outline of the History of Friends in Council, Quincy, Illinois,* p. 5. This brochure was written by Mrs. Denman in 1872.

turned to Plato and continued with him for a second year, during one month of which Dr. Jones, of Jacksonville, visited in Quincy and attended all of the meetings. After two years with Plato Mrs. Denman could say:

I think at our parting we were ready to adopt Buckle's idea, "that mental pleasures are more ennobling than physical ones." We regretted that we could not together finish the work, but accepted the idea that "by enlarged intellectual culture, especially by philosophical studies, the mind at last comes to pursue truth for its own sake; to esteem it a duty to emancipate ourselves from party spirit, prejudice and passion and to cultivate love of truth, tolerance and patience through all opposition." [9]

It is possible to conclude that Plato gave these women the attitude characterized by the above quotation. It is also possible, even more likely, that they took with them to their study of Plato needs and desires which Plato helped to bring to conscious expression. Friends in Council was no sewing circle. It was founded with an intellectual motive and its program was far from that offered by the conventional Monday afternoon club today. Mrs. S. H. Emery, Jr., wrote years later (1878), describing the objective of the club in somewhat Platonic terms:

Friends in Council was summoned into existence to serve a purpose other than a trivial or merely temporary one. It is an association formed by women for their own improvement, and its aims are of broader scope than such as may afford variety to monotonous lives, or may meet the immediate and evanescent wants of the passing day and hour. It aspires to the office of awakening in its members and constantly re-invigorating within them a desire for personal, progressive growth in the direction of whatever is noble, beautiful, just and true. The end of this organization is to encourage and stimulate to the performance

[9] *Ibid.,* pp. 5–6.

of such work as lies in the range of woman's best faculties, intellectual, moral and practical; work which shall result in lifting its members above that which is puerile and perishable in life to the ultimate attainment of all which constitutes a symmetrical and complete womanhood.[10]

To get even more perspective on the club and its purpose, one may refer to the account which Miss Mary B. Bull wrote in 1916. In this she paid tribute to Mrs. Denman but at the same time described the essential purpose of the organization.

Looking back after the lapse of years, Mrs. Denman appears as one of the leaders in the important movements of the day, especially in advancing the higher education of women. She discerned the need in women's lives of intellectual interests and opportunity for individual culture, not only for the enrichment of the personal life, but as preparation for greater usefulness. . . . Her reliance upon the inner forces, was the power which moulded the society in its plastic days. To her clear purpose with its firm renouncements, stamping its ineffaceable impression upon Friends in Council in its youth, more than to any other influence, the society owes its continued existence and singleness of aim.[11]

While the reading of the Platonic dialogues continued only for two full years, this should not be interpreted as meaning that the club had lost its interest either in Plato or in philosophy. It was not until the 1890s that philosophy began to lose the esteem of Friends in Council. Alcott appeared before the club on numerous occasions while visiting either the Lorenzo Bulls or the Denmans, and special sessions were held in his honor. Hiram K. Jones was a frequent visitor, often staying two or more weeks at a time visiting the Denmans. Papers on Plato and Neoplatonism were read,

[10] *Ibid.*, p. 7.   [11] *Ibid.*, p. 18.

and philosophy in its various forms played an influential role even when other subjects, literary, artistic, and historical, were added. Part of the program for two years was given over to the study of Cousin's *History of Modern Philosophy*. One year the relation between mind and body occupied the club's attention. In 1877–78 the philosophy of history was studied. One section in 1888–89 was devoted to the study of English thinkers and in 1889–90, one to evolution as represented in the works of Haeckel, Darwin, Huxley, and Spencer. Somewhat characteristic was the program of 1879–80, devoted to modern science, in which the following topics were considered: "Method of Science" (Mill, Whewell, Jevons), "Definition and Object of Physics," "Theories Concerning the Ultimate Structure of Matter," "The New Chemistry," "Biology" (Cook, LeConte, Tyndall), "The Descent of Life" (Darwin, Haeckel, Galton, Huxley, Mivart), "Mental Physiology" (Lewes, Bain, Martineau, Lotze), "Cosmogony" (Spencer, Huxley), "The Theistic Philosophy of Evolution" (Gray).

The intellectual quality of the group was also demonstrated by the type of person it produced. Two of the members were Mrs. Anna B. McMahan and Cora A. Benneson. Mrs. McMahan, a graduate of Bryn Mawr, became a lecturer on English literature, wrote books on Wordsworth, Byron, and Shelley, and contributed to literary journals as well as serving as editorial writer for the *Chicago Tribune* after her husband died.[12] Miss Benneson was a graduate of the University of Michigan with B.A., M.A., and LL.B. degrees, and was an undergraduate friend of Alice Freeman

[12] Refer to Orie Latham Hatcher, *Anna B. McMahan* (privately printed in pamphlet form).

Palmer. She was admitted to the bar in both Michigan and
Illinois. In addition to writing for magazines she read occasional papers before the American Association for the
Advancement of Science ("Executive Discretion in the
United States," "Federal Guarantees for Maintaining Republican Government in the States," and "The Power of
Our Courts to Interpret the Constitution" were among
them), and was made secretary of the social and economic
science section in 1900.[13] Detailed information is lacking on
many other members of Friends in Council, but the record of
the two mentioned is suggestive of the quality of mind which
the organization produced. Friends in Council was an organization with serious intent and should not be confused with
some of its modern descendants. The ultimate objective was
to help each member develop a philosophical point of view
for himself. Characteristic of the independence of judgment
which members exercised is the following quotation from a
short paper on "Sacrifice" which Mrs. John McFadon read
to the group sometime during the 1870s:

As this is a good place to air one's opinions, I take this opportunity to let the "Phil. Club" know just where I stand. I am
often told by them, I can not be a philosopher, unless I believe
in the "Trinity." Then I can remain just where I am; for I
shall not give up my personality in order to be a philosopher, or
any thing else; unless I can do it understandingly. I believe entirely in the "One and Many, Unlimited, Universal," unlimited
by any threeness or 5ness, or 7ness or divided by any arbitrary
rules or laws whatever. I am not obliged to swallow down whole
any old heathen philosopher merely because he is old. I believe

[13] Refer to Mary Esther Trueblood, "Cora Agnes Benneson," in Julia
Ward Howe and Mary H. Graves (eds.), *Sketches of Representative
Women of New England* (Boston, New England Historical Publishing
Co., 1904).

this "Trinity" is only a remnant of barbarism, and the worship of a false God.[14]

It is enlightening to refer to the footnote which Mrs. McFadon made to her remark about swallowing "heathen philosophers": "For all we want of any author, is just enough to make us think; if more, you become 'imitators' merely, like Plato's poets, in his Republic. In this way does thinking become a 'lost art.' " There was real independence in the western mind of this period and there was also a desire for self-expression which interest in the philosophic greats could only enkindle, not stifle.

The numerous contacts between Quincy and Jacksonville had much to do with the predominant influence which Platonic philosophy had in Quincy, both in and out of Friends in Council. The two cities had long had cultural contacts. When the medical department of Illinois College was established in 1843, two of the four men appointed to positions were Quincy physicians, David Prince and Daniel Stahl. William H. Collins, a Congregational minister and writer on philosophical subjects, received his B.A. from Illinois College, owned and edited the Jacksonville *Journal* for a period of time, and later became a trustee of the college. Lorenzo Bull also served for a time on the board. So close were the cultural ties between the two towns that in 1853, when Illinois College was having financial difficulties, President Julian Sturtevant suggested that the college be moved to Quincy because of its cultural similarity and greater potential growth. Sorosis of Jacksonville and Friends in Council corresponded and exchanged papers. When the American Akademe was started, Quincy provided one of the

[14] MS, "Friends in Council. Scrapbook with Programs up to 1915–16," p. 75.

largest out-of-town membership lists in the organization. Mr. and Mrs. S. H. Emery, Jr., Edward McClure, Miss Anna McClure, Cora A. Benneson, Rev. and Mrs. C. F. Bradley, Mr. and Mrs. James Woodruff, Mrs. Lorenzo Bull, Dr. and Mrs. Reuben Woods, Sheridan Waite, William H. Collins, Mrs. Ella P. Rogers, and Mrs. Rose Nelson Clapp all became members and many of them read papers before the Jacksonville group.

Even more important than the cultural homogeneity of the two cities were the personal friendships between Quincy and Jacksonville people. Mrs. Denman was a particular friend of Mrs. J. O. King, Mrs. Elizur Wolcott, and Miss Louise Fuller, the three original members, along with Hiram K. Jones, of the Plato Club in Jacksonville. She visited in their homes and they in hers. Miss Fuller lived in Quincy from around 1866 to 1869 and was one of the members of Friends in Council. She may have been responsible originally for suggesting that Mrs. Denman and Friends in Council read Plato. Dr. Jones visited in Quincy on many occasions and stayed as long as a month at a time during which discussion of Platonic themes was common.

In 1869, Friends in Council, after an experimental period of three years, decided to enlarge its membership, setting a maximum limit of thirty-five members. This meant greater diversity of interest, and a varied program took the place of the constant study of Plato. In later years the organization planned its program in sections, providing a wider range of subjects for the members. The philosophical interest was continued, but Plato never again became the sole interest of the organization. This was undoubtedly a disappointment to Mrs. Denman, who was forced to carry on her Platonic studies either alone or along with another group she may have formed. In any case, she was an important figure in a third club which was started in 1871; this club included men, and its leader was Samuel H. Emery, Jr.

How profound Mrs. Denman's Platonic studies were is difficult to say because nothing of what she wrote (her writings were probably not extensive, in any event) is available. That her study was purposive is not to be doubted. She visited Jacksonville on occasion, with the particular object of attending Plato Club meetings. Jones came to be, during the 1870s, a more than frequent visitor of the Denmans in Quincy. Mrs. Denman supplemented her own study of Plato by notes of the Jacksonville meetings supplied to her by Mrs. King. Miss Louise Fuller indicates that, in addition to Friends in Council, Mrs. Denman formed a second group for the study of Plato during the 1860s. The following quotation suggests this: "Mrs. King took notes of the readings and comments and sent them to Mrs. Sarah Denman in Quincy where a circle of friends, mostly teachers, read with the help of the notes, the books they were reading in Jacksonville." [15]

This quotation refers to the 1860s and hence the group mentioned can hardly be confused with the mixed club which Emery later organized. The fact that Miss Fuller speaks of the group as being composed of teachers would seem to eliminate Friends in Council, which was made up largely of married women who were not teachers. In all likelihood, therefore, Mrs. Denman had her own study group where Plato was read and the notes of Mrs. King discussed. Supposing this to be true, just what of Plato they read and discussed is not easy to determine. We do know that Friends in Council, during its second year of study, read the *Char-*

[15] "The Plato Club," *Journal of the American Akademe*, V (1890), 20.

mides, Symposium, and *Philebus.* Whether the private group went over the same or other dialogues is difficult to know. Nor is it possible to find out how long the group lasted. We do know that Mrs. Denman was still receiving notes from Mrs. King in 1879, for Friends in Council has in its possession four books of notes in Mrs. Denman's handwriting running from 1873 to 1879. At first sight these notes appear to be ones which Mrs. Denman made herself after studying the dialogues. Closer scrutiny, however, leads to the conclusion that these are but copies of Mrs. King's. In one place is a notation: "no notes, Mrs. K. absent." In another is: "notes by Louise Fuller." Still another has: "Dr. Jones called for the opinion of the class on the subject of immortality." Others have such as: "No reading. Dr. not well" or "Dr. in Quincy," with nothing but dates to indicate that there were no meetings when Dr. Jones was absent or indisposed. One or two are reports of conversations between Alcott and Jones and two are summaries of talks by Denton J. Snider on Hegelian philosophy and on Goethe. These could hardly have taken place in Quincy since there is no record of Snider's ever having been there and there is no record of Alcott and Jones visiting there at that particular time. It seems quite clear, therefore, that these were originally Mrs. King's notes copied by Mrs. Denman for her own later reference.[16]

These notes provide some indication of the type of discussion in which the women of Jacksonville and Quincy engaged. The available notes of Mrs. Denman are on the *First Alcibiades,* running from June 27 to August 2, 1873; on the *Republic,* from August 30, 1873, to November 18, 1876; on

[16] This has been confirmed by the author after comparing the notes of Mrs. King possessed by Mrs. A. E. McVitty of Princeton, N.J. and those of Mrs. Denman. It is a strange coincidence that the only surviving notes of these two women are for the same years.

the *Timaeus,* from November 25, 1876, to March 30, 1878; on the *Critias,* from April 13 to October 26, 1878; on the *Meno,* from November 2 to November 9, 1878; and from November 23 to December 21, 1878; and on the *Euthydemus,* from December 28, 1878, to January 18, 1879. The notes were largely exegetical in form. Page numbers, chapters, and sections were often included along with the date.

Reference to a single day's notes gives some knowledge of their quality. The following, taken at random, for the meeting of March 30, 1878, which closed the study of the *Timaeus,* is typical, being neither the shortest nor the longest, the most nor the least profound.

We find in the constitution and nature of man an epitome of the universe. The trifold nature of man is also like the universe—heaven, earth and hell—intelligence, moral and desiderative in man. The harmony of the universe is found in the counterpoise of the extremes by the middle term. There could not be harmony any more than in music without the extremes of concord and discord. The musician is effecting the logic of the universe in reconciling the two. So man must reconcile the two extremes in his nature; then he is in order, the will allied to the intelligence and the desires subordinate. The monastic order would annihilate the desires and so hell would be annihilated. Others think that evil must always exist—this is the maintenance of the duality of the universe. We shall realize more wisdom in finding the *Divine idea*—that all God's works are good. As the child cannot accept the thought of the philosopher, or the music of the masters, so we cannot accept the works of the Creator.

Coldness becomes absolute, the otherness of the heat, and will destroy life. Either can be carried to such extremes that there is a positive somewhat in them. Would it be better if the physical constitution of nature were heat only, and may we not infer that evil is a necessity? Is the universe right or is it pervaded by error? What would it be if all evil were eliminated, if man had only intelligence? Plato says that the supreme is a kingly intellect in a royal soul.

We must see the threeness of the universe and of the human soul to be their eternal constitution. We shall not succeed in abolishing the trinity. Perhaps the plane on which our earth is, is below the middle, we are more in hell than in heaven. This world we are in is the best place to seek the true, the beautiful and the good. The undying soul can go down into physics and nature; these are the instruments of mind. It is a perpetual miracle that an undying nature can pursue a mortal existence, but the greater wonder is that we can exist here immortally. The natural man is only conscious of the mortal but another has his spiritual consciousness opened and he has immortal realizations. We can participate of both. We can pass through the veil and still see only the mortal. We shall ever stand in the duality of the ideal and actual. We do not change our relation to the universe by laying off the body. The mortal nature in man assimilates us to the divine. We are not to chose either exclusively. The unity of these is found in the culture of both.[17]

Mrs. Denman played an important role in Quincy by leading the feminine movement for self-education and self-expression. She gave it a decidedly philosophical cast because of her own interest in Plato and the Platonic organon as it emanated from the midwestern Platonic teacher, Hiram K. Jones. Although she provided Quincy with its first active philosophic group, her leadership was soon superseded by that of S. H. Emery, Jr., who ultimately brought national recognition to Quincy through his prominence at the Concord School of Philosophy and through the few writings of his which were published.

Emery was born at Taunton, Massachusetts, August 3,

[17] MS, Notes of Mrs. Sarah Denman, III, 127–29.

1840. He was the son of a Congregational minister of first rank, good fortune from his standpoint because at that time no family background contributed more to the cultural development of children than that of the liberal minister. When Emery was fifteen, his parents moved to Quincy and he went to Harvard, having finished his preliminary work at Bristol Academy. He transferred to Amherst for a second year after which he went to Quincy to spend the summer with his family. He secured a temporary position at the Comstock Stove Foundry and liked it so much that he chose not to return to college in the fall. He stayed with this firm until 1879 when, along with his brother-in-law, Edward McClure, he returned east to attend law school at Harvard. He received the LL.B. degree in 1882 (Amherst had awarded him an honorary M.A. degree in 1872) and, although he lived in Concord, he practiced law intermittently in Boston. His philosophical interests were so engrossing during this period that he had no time to build up a legal practice. With the demise of the Concord School in 1888 he returned to business in Quincy. He became vice-president of the Quincy Paper Company and later, its manager, when this company combined with the American Show Board Company. He was also president of the Electric Wheel Company and vice-president of the Channon-Emery Stove Company. Emery's business interests always rested lightly on his shoulders, for he had the ability to make quick, accurate decisions. Among other virtues were his commanding presence and his balanced judgment. He was described as follows: "Tall and straight as an arrow, of unusually fine presence, he is a man who would command attention in any assemblage. By reason of his broad and comprehensive learning, he is a strong and convincing writer and a ready speaker. While he holds positive opinions and is frank in expressing them, he is fair and considerate in all things." [18]

As was said earlier, Emery's philosophical interest was inspired by Emerson near the middle of the 1860s. Emerson particularly recommended the Platonic dialogues to Emery, who read them with care and discrimination. Emerson also suggested Stirling's *Secret of Hegel* as worthy of study, for he was reading it himself at the time. Plato first engulfed Emery, but as time went on Hegel assumed greater importance principally because of his reading of the *Journal of Speculative Philosophy*, his correspondence with Harris, and later (after 1879), his personal friendship with Harris. That Emery was no mere superficial reader of philosophical classics is clear both through what others said about him and through his own writings. Before Harris had even met Emery he spoke of him as a "young giant in philosophy." [19] Along with a notice of Emery's death which appeared in the Springfield (Massachusetts) *Republican* and was reprinted in the Quincy *Whig* for February 6, 1906, was a tribute to Emery by someone who knew him well at Concord. Since F. H. Sanborn was writing for this paper it is undoubtedly his judgment of Emery. It said:

He had clearness of perception, equanimity of temper and dignity of manner, and held to his own view of philosophy with modest firmness, without often intruding it, or making it, as some of the debators would, a sort of battleflag in the strife of opinions. Indeed, he was properly joined with those men elder in years, Alcott, Emerson, Harris and others, whose conception of philosophizing was a conversation and a calm suggestion, rather than a wrangle of Scotch metaphysicians. His very cool-

[18] David F. Wilcox (ed.), *Representative Men and Homes, Quincy, Illinois* (Quincy, Volk, Jones, and McMein, 1899), p. 27.
[19] MS, Diary of Thomas M. Johnson, June 14, 1876.

ness and precision of manner, the fruit of admirable method in his arrangement of thoughts, gave calmness to the discussion and kept within bounds some of the wide wandering hypotheses which such gatherings are apt to witness.

Emery's philosophical library was not large, nothing to compare with Jones' library in Jacksonville or Johnson's in Osceola. Nevertheless he did have materials with which to work. He had two sets of Jowett's translation of Plato's dialogues, two sets of Hegel's complete works, a variety of books about Plato and Hegel, and a miscellaneous collection of the works of Samuel Butler, Fénelon, Coleridge, Josephus, Plutarch, Aristotle, Henry More, Hume, Locke, Van Helmont, Marcus Aurelius, Darwin, Mill, Spencer, Fichte, and Montaigne, among others. He had a bound set of the *Journal of Speculative Philosophy*, and the German Philosophical Classics edited by G. S. Morris.

Emery's study of Plato began in the 1860s. It was not, however, until the early 1870s that the Plato Club was organized under his leadership. Although its motive was the same as that of the club in Jacksonville, the Quincy Plato Club was more informal, records were never kept, and hence no membership list is available. It first met at the Quincy Female Seminary, often known as Miss Chapin's School because Caroline and Mary Chapin were its administrators. Both of these women were members of the Plato Club as well as members of Friends in Council. The club met on Thursday evenings and in addition to Emery and the Chapin sisters it included, at one time or another, Mr. and Mrs. C. H. Bull, Mrs. John McFadon, Mrs. Lorenzo Bull, Mrs. Ebenezer Baldwin, Dr. R. K. Rutherford, Edward McClure, Mrs. Emery, Mrs. Rutherford, and Mrs. Denman. The average attendance was said to be between eight and ten. The Quincy

Female Seminary ceased operation around 1873 and this necessitated finding another place in which to meet. Mrs. McFadon's home was used most of the time, but the group often met at Emery's home and elsewhere.

Almost all of these people had a background favorable to the study of philosophy, or at least a serious and constant interest in it. Mrs. McFadon had been influenced by William Ellery Channing while studying in Boston. Dr. Rutherford was a physician and scientist, known widely for his demonstrations in physics and chemistry. Both of the Mesdames Bull had received a good education and had traveled widely. Second to Emery in real philosophical ability was his brother-in-law, Edward McClure, who lived with the Emerys. McClure, born in Malden, Massachusetts, had gone to Pittsburgh early and secured a job with a railroad. He subsequently established one of the first coke companies and this was a great financial success. Having built up a substantial fortune in a short time, he retired and went to Quincy to live with the Emerys, and gave his attention largely to philosophy. He was a great reader and devoured philosophical volumes with ease. He was a regular attendant at the Concord School but never wrote or appeared in public to discuss philosophic themes. Philosophy to him was a source of personal enjoyment, neither a means of living nor a gospel to preach. In small, informal groups, his opinions were always held in high regard.

Characteristic of the seriousness of the various members of the group was Mrs. Baldwin. She, like Emery and McClure, became interested in Hegel as well as Plato. When she went on a trip to Colorado and New Mexico with Dr. E. B. Montgomery in 1879 to recover her health, she took along a copy of Stirling's *Secret of Hegel* and completely mastered it, not being content to desert philosophy, even for her health. She was a member of a group which met as early as 1873, at Mrs. Lorenzo Bull's home, to read Mill's *System of Logic*. These people had real zest for philosophy. They were less spiritually motivated than the members of the Jacksonville club but they were equally serious and in certain regards their philosophic interests had broader scope.

The most productive mind in Quincy was Emery. His lead in the Plato Club was an outgrowth of a significant interest in the Platonic system. Emery's mind was less partial than Hiram K. Jones'; the result was that he had a somewhat more scholarly interest in the dialogues. His most important contribution was his analysis of the *Parmenides*. It first appeared in the *Journal of Speculative Philosophy* (VI [1872], 279–84). He subsequently revised and enlarged it, read it before the American Akademe in Jacksonville, and had it printed in its *Journal* (III [1887], 147–67). William Torrey Harris, in an editor's note prefacing Emery's article said: "In Quincy and Jacksonville (Illinois) there are two flourishing philosophical clubs that have been prosecuting vigorously the study of Plato. The bravery that attacks Plato, and especially the *Parmenides*, deserves the highest admiration." [20]

In this early interpretation of the *Parmenides* (Emery was thirty-two at the time), he conceived Plato's object to be that of showing the depth of the Eleatic point of view as against the Socratic one, based largely on Parmenides' explanation of philosophical method in the second part of the dialogue. Emery interpreted the dialogue as presenting three basic hypotheses: (1) that the One is an indefinite immediate and as such forecloses on the possibility of the Many

[20] *Journal of Speculative Philosophy*, VI (1872), 279.

existing; (2) that the One is self-determining and includes the Many; (3) that the One is both indeterminate and self-determining, best understood as becoming in eternity and as self-identical. This third hypothesis was thought by Emery to be a synthesis of the first two and Plato's real point of view. There seems to be little doubt that Emery was greatly influenced in this analysis by Hegel's interpretation of Plato, which he quoted. Plato was, even at this date in Emery's career, an historical example of what ultimately is better expressed by nineteenth-century idealism. Emery confessed to this Hegelian bias in the discussion which followed the revised analysis which he read at Jacksonville in 1887. He said:

It was almost twenty years ago that I first read the *Parmenides.* Mr. Emerson came out to Quincy at my suggestion to lecture. I was interested in his thought, and I asked him what book to read. He told me if I wanted intellectual gymnastic to read Stirling's *Secret of Hegel.* I have not mastered it yet. Some time after I started a class in Plato to see if it was any easier. The brief paper on the *Parmenides* published in the *Journal of Speculative Philosophy* was the result. Since then I have worked at it, and last year wrote this paper. The way in which I got at it was through the *Secret of Hegel,* the history of philosophy, and Plato's other dialogues. To take up this dialogue without preparation would be idle industry.[21]

This later interpretation suffered less from Emery's increasingly Hegelian bias than did the earlier one. Harris spoke of this paper as "the most profound treatment of the *Parmenides* that I know of in any language."[22] It was a careful analysis and placed the dialogue in the perspective of the philosophical issues alive in Plato's time. Emery was

[21] *Journal of the American Akademe,* III (1887), 168–69.
[22] *Ibid.,* p. 169.

in agreement with E. Munk, who argued for a logical sequence of the Platonic dialogues which would place the *Parmenides* first. Emery's definition of philosophy indicates something of his metaphysical predilection. He said, "Philosophy as a special form of thought is an attempt to state the supreme principle of the universe and to apply the principle in explanation of all that is." [23] By this time Emery had come to believe that Socrates rather than Parmenides was the spokesman for Plato. He had earlier been deceived by the dialectical method of Plato to the extent that he believed Socrates to be the supporter of positions which he was merely setting up for Parmenides to attack. Plato, he argued now, was attempting to find some reconciliation between the Eleatic and Heraclitean points of view, and thus developed the first real system of philosophy, of which the *Parmenides* was the earliest expression. He now saw three basic positions considered and denominated them pantheism (only the One is), dualism (only the Many are), and monism (both the One and the Many are). The discussion thus hinged on the problem of the existence of the One. Plato had six positive and three negative arguments to prove the existence of the One as a self-determining, all-inclusive universal. The final conclusion at which Emery arrived was similar to that of his early analysis, namely, that Plato argued for the existence of a One and also a Many, not separate but fundamentally in union in the act of becoming. The superiority of this second analysis over the first lies in its greater comprehensiveness and clarity of expression. Criticism could be made of Emery's position from the standpoint of Platonic scholarship today, but for the period in which it was made it was a superior accomplishment.

[23] *Ibid.*, p. 148.

Emery wrote occasionally for the *Journal of Speculative Philosophy*. In 1873 he was concerned over personal immortality and wrote a letter to the editor criticizing the position of A. E. Kroeger, who had argued that only an empirical proof would be sufficient to establish its existence. Emery held that this was impossible, that an a priori basis alone could be found for it, that even this was difficult, and that perhaps all we could defend would be immortality through the participation of the particular in the universal. In 1877 he wrote an article entitled, "Does Formal Logic Explain Active Processes?" In this he argued that the understanding has no way of establishing the existence of motion, that reason alone can assure us of its certainty. In 1881 he wrote an article on Lucretius, holding that the great atomist had stated the doctrine of materialism and natural evolution more effectively than had been done by the more recent defenders of the viewpoint. Harris regarded this analysis of Lucretius as superior to one of his own published in 1873. Emery wrote an article on "Culture and Discipline" which appeared in *The Western*, for June, 1877. He also wrote an essay, "The Elective Affinities," which had been delivered in lecture form at Concord in 1885.[24] To the writer's knowledge these are all the published writings of Emery. He, of course, presided at the sessions of the Concord School of Philosophy and participated in its discussions as well as lecturing on such subjects as "System in Philosophy." Copies of these lectures, except the one mentioned above, no longer appear to be in existence.

Emery's study of Hegel began about the same time as his study of Plato. He was one of the early subscribers to the

[24] It was published in F. B. Sanborn (ed.), *The Life and Genius of Goethe* (Boston, Ticknor, 1886), pp. 251–89.

Journal of Speculative Philosophy. As time went on, his allegiance to Hegel increased, although at first he had feared he would never understand him. The materials which he regularly read in the *Journal of Speculative Philosophy,* however, encouraged his increasing devotion to Hegel rather than to Plato. As early as 1868, Harris was writing to argue that Plato and the Greeks were unable to present philosophy systematically, as compared with Hegel.[25] This constant literary nourishment from St. Louis undoubtedly had much to do with lessening the influence Hiram K. Jones exerted on Plato's behalf on his intermittent visits to Quincy. If Emery had completely had his way Quincy might have had a club for the study of Hegel rather than Plato, but his own feeling of incompetence and the interest of others turned the organizational tide in Quincy in favor of Plato. By 1875 Emery himself was definitely more interested in Hegel. He had corresponded with Harris and impressed the editor-philosopher with his keen discriminative philosophical powers. One problem he faced was inadequate preparation in German. He bought Hegel in the original but found himself unable to master the text. He therefore wrote to Harris asking if he could borrow Brokmeyer's translation of the "Logic" and have a copy made for his own use. This met with Harris' approval as well as Brokmeyer's, and in 1875 he succeeded in completing the project. This was no easy job, copying by hand what, in other translations, is a two volume work. Emery tried two women copyists but each gave it up after a short time. Then he discovered Sally Williams, the daughter of a circuit judge, who had just graduated from preparatory school and who had seen the necessity for

[25] *Journal of Speculative Philosophy,* II (1868), 1–3.

accuracy through copying legal work for her father. Emery
questioned her on her tenacity, but she told him she had
Scotch blood and that she would finish the job whatever the
obstacles. The manuscript was in sections in large folders.
Sally was hired to do the work for one dollar per section.
Two had been finished by the previous copyists, and she received twenty-five dollars when the job was completed; hence
the manuscript must have been in twenty-seven sections. It
was a laborious task and it took Sally three months to complete the job, but it was carefully done, for she and her sister
proofread it to be certain that it was exact.[26] Thus it was
that Emery succeeded in getting an English translation of
one of Hegel's major works. The Logic was a textbook for
him from that time on. Within three years Emery became a
convert to the philosophy of Hegel. In March, 1878, he
wrote to Harris that Dr. Jones had been visiting in Quincy
for a week and had become interested in Hegel and would
read him. The result was that Emery had a second copy of
the Brokmeyer translation made at Jones' request and sent
it to him a few months later. The writer has been unable to
ascertain who made this copy, although it is clear that it was
not Miss Williams, for finishing one copy was quite enough
for her. She decided teaching was both more pleasant and
more remunerative than copying a manuscript which held
little or no meaning for her.[27] Louis Block and Dr. Jones
began reading Hegel in the fall of 1878. Block wrote to Harris in December, 1878, "Dr. Jones and I are hard at work

[26] This information was contributed by Miss Williams in personal conversation.
[27] Dr. Jones' copy is in the library at Illinois College at Jacksonville.
Emery's copy was said to be in his daughter's (Mrs. Constance Ellis')
attic in Quincy, but the author was not able to find it. Mrs. Ellis has
since died.

in the large Logic of Hegel. He uses the translation obtained from Mr. Emery, and I the German. We see daylight and are getting somewhat accustomed to that region."

Emery's missionary zeal for Hegel was not limited to Quincy and Jacksonville. It extended to Boston, for in 1879, when he went east to attend law school, he took his copy of Brokmeyer's translation and tried to impress its importance upon a circle of philosophically-minded people there. William James, in his essay on Thomas Davidson, refers to this event as happening the year before Davidson arrived. He said:

The previous year we had gone over a good part of Hegel's Larger Logic, under the self-constituted leadership of two young business men from Illinois, who had become enthusiastic Hegelians and, knowing almost no German, had actually possessed themselves of a manuscript translation of the entire three volumes of Logic, made by an extraordinary Pomeranian immigrant, named Brokmeyer. These disciples were leaving business for the law and studying at the Harvard law-school; but they saw the whole universe through Hegelian spectacles, and a more admirable *homo unius libri* than one of them, with his three big folios of Hegelian manuscript, I have never had the good fortune to know.[28]

According to James, this should have occurred about 1872. James was undoubtedly wrong in placing this event so early; Davidson didn't arrive in Boston until 1875. But he is probably still further wrong, as he often was when it came to dates, for Emery and McClure (undoubtedly the men referred to) did not arrive until 1879. James may have been confused in his chronology because of the succession of clubs to which he belonged, at one of which the study of

[28] William James, *Memories and Studies* (New York, Longmans, Green, 1911), pp. 81–82.

Hegel took place. James, along with Peirce and Wright, belonged to a Metaphysical Club in the early 1870s. He also belonged to another club (which may have been the same one, reorganized) by 1876. A third club was started in 1881 by Harris. It is undoubtedly the second of these clubs at which the study of Hegel took place, and during 1879, rather than earlier. In any case, the point is that Emery and McClure took the gospel of Hegel east and played a part in turning philosophical discussion in Boston and Cambridge toward Hegel and the idealistic tradition.

Quincy philosophy had little of the scholastic emphasis and the prophetic quality of that in Jacksonville. The Quincy people were equally sincere in their devotion to philosophical ideas. Their clubs served a similar need and a similar class of people. Yet it was more difficult to keep the Quincy people within the bounds of a closely-knit system. Plato was generally more influential, but Hegel also had a hearing. The club for the study of Mill's Logic also acquired a following. Quincy's philosophical groups were not dominated by any one figure such as Jones in Jacksonville or Harris in St. Louis. Quincy was an outpost of philosophy, and its citizens acquired an interest in various streams of thought. It would be going too far to say that the Quincy people had a truly cosmopolitan interest in philosophy, yet their range of interest was broader than that of people in other cities where there was a more clearly systematized and elaborated point of view. Quincy was responsible for no new developments in philosophy; instead it absorbed the spirit of movements which were started elsewhere and made those movements a part of its own cultural life.

Organized study of philosophy in Quincy was of shorter duration than in Jacksonville or St. Louis. This was largely caused by the death of one of the leaders and by the departure, for Concord, of another. Mrs. Denman's death in 1881 was a great loss to the cultural life of the city. Emery's departure for Concord in 1879, along with that of McClure, meant the removal of the dominant masculine figures in the movement. It is true that Emery and McClure returned in 1888, but this was at a time when other interests were taking the place of philosophical ones. Literary interests were in the ascendancy, even at Concord. Goethe, Shakespeare, Browning—these names took the place of Plato, Aristotle, and Hegel. Philosophy did not die out in Quincy with the loss of its chief protagonists, but it did lose its organizational stability. When Emery returned, even he gave less attention to the vigorous study of philosophical classics than formerly. He was now preoccupied with business, and in this his was but a single example of how the rising industrial order, together with the growing interest in general and psychological literature, made the continuance of philosophical study groups a vestige of a passing era rather than the expression of a new one.

CHAPTER V

THE SAGE OF THE OSAGE

As the westward movement gathered momentum in the nineteenth century, population was concentrated on the banks of navigable streams before railroads became the great medium of commerce. The early towns in Kansas and Nebraska were settlements on the banks of the Missouri River. In like manner, but to a lesser degree, western Missouri was inhabited by people who followed along the banks of the Osage, an alternative and less traveled route which led into southern Kansas, east and south of Topeka. Osceola, on the Osage, was an active commercial center by the middle of the century, for it served as a mart for the agricultural products of the surrounding region, and steamboats plied from there to St. Louis. Being in a border state, however, it suffered both from the reign of terror which followed the sacking of Lawrence, Kansas, in 1856, and also from the Civil War, when the town was nearly razed. These tragedies reduced Osceola to the status of a conventional village, for even though it was a county seat, it never rose again to its pre-Civil War status. Today its population is somewhere around 1,000, its square surrounded by a few commercial establishments. It is generally lacking in the enterprise characteristic of similar towns north and east. Osceola is no ghost town, but neither is it, nor has it been since the Civil War, a center of progress and culture. In view of this, the story which follows is all the more remarkable, for Osceola, because of the residence of Thomas M. Johnson, came to be regarded as one of the centers of Platonic philosophy and scholarship in America, quite out of proportion to the energy, the education, and the culture of the majority of its residents. Of the midwestern men who made a contribution to philosophy during the period, none gave more concerted attention to scholarship than did Johnson. If it can be said that Harris was the greatest promoter of philosophy and Jones the greatest Platonic philosopher, it can equally well be said that Johnson was the greatest scholar and bibliophile.

The westward movement brought with it many people of substance. Among these were Waldo Johnson and his wife, who migrated to Osceola from Clarksburg, Virginia, in the early 1840s. They brought prominence to the town. Johnson became one of the leading political figures in the state. He was a circuit judge in the early 1850s and was elected United States senator in March, 1861. In August of the same year he resigned from his office because he was essentially a state rights man, although he had been elected on an antisecession platform. He joined the Confederate Army, became a colonel, served in the Confederate Senate, and was a personal adviser to Jefferson Davis. When the war was over he served on the peace commission and later (1875) was president of the Missouri Constitutional Convention. He was an eminently successful lawyer and left a fair-sized estate to his four sons when he died in 1884. One of the sons became a cattle broker, one a railroad engineer, and the other two lawyers.

Thomas Moore Johnson, one of the sons destined for the law, was born at Osceola, March 30, 1851. His early education was interrupted because of the Civil War; he studied first in Osceola and then later at Clarksburg, West Virginia, and at Hamilton, Ontario, where the family had fled by a circuitous route after the fall of Richmond. By the age of fourteen he was back in Osceola, where he stayed until he enrolled in the University of Notre Dame. His brother, William T. Johnson, had preceded him there, had been converted to Catholicism, and subsequently, while active in Kansas City as a prominent layman as well as lawyer, became a Knight of St. Gregory, the highest lay honor conferred by the pope. Thomas never shared his brother's enthusiasm for Catholicism, but he stayed in Notre Dame until he had finished the requirements for graduation in 1871.[1] He then returned home, studied law under his father, and was admitted to the bar in 1872, although his attention to law thereafter was sporadic and inconsequential. He did serve as prosecuting attorney for two terms (1874–76 and 1898–1900), but each time he refused to run for reelection. He spent a year in Nevada, Missouri (1873), serving an apprenticeship in law, and two years in Clayton, Missouri, as editor of a newspaper. His legal practice in Osceola was limited because his sole purpose in following the law was to keep financially solvent in order to acquire philosophy books. His one great desire was to study philosophy and within this field to further the cause of one particular movement, Platonism. His father, a practical man, did everything he could to dissuade him from spending so much time on what he called "musty volumes," and even offered special incen-

[1] For some reason the B.A. degree was not awarded until 1876. He was awarded the M.A. degree by the same institution in 1892.

tives to inspire greater interest in the law, but to no avail. Philosophy was, to Thomas, all-consuming and his legal practice was a means rather than an end.

Johnson was something of a misanthrope, although he demonstrated occasional interest in civic problems. He served as mayor for a period of ten years. He was on the board of education for a much longer period, part of the time as president; he insisted that Latin be taught in the public schools and offered a yearly prize for achievement in Latin as an incentive for its study. But these things were secondary, as was travel. Few were the occasions when he left Osceola for more than a day or two; he was quoted as saying that "he always liked to be places but he didn't like to go places." His close friends in the community were few, his best ones invariably his correspondents. Local people viewed him with respect, mingled with wonder. He was often regarded as a snob since, being both nearsighted and hard of hearing, he appeared to ignore people when he passed them on the street. Even if he had not suffered from these physical disabilities, he would still have been remembered as eccentric, for he could be observed twice a day reading a pocket-size edition of some classical author as he walked to the express office to pick up new books for his growing collection. Despite his lack of sufficient contact with the outside world and failing health in his later years, his persistent study raised him to a position of eminence as a scholar and bibliophile. Long before his death of arteriosclerosis on March 2, 1919, he had been commonly referred to as "The Sage of the Osage."

Johnson first developed an interest in philosophy at Notre Dame, although he had acquired the habit of reading much earlier. Late in his career he said: "I cannot remember when

I could not read, or, in fact, was not reading. I do not know when or where I learned to read; I have been told I was taught at home. Be that as it may, my desire to read from my childhood was insatiable, and is still undiminished." [2] This habit of reading led him to the library stacks at Notre Dame, where he found sources which influenced him through life. His first acquaintance with philosophy dates from the spring of 1870, when he was browsing in the library and came upon some old volumes of the *Classical Journal*, published in London from 1810 to 1829.[3] The first item he noticed was the "Chaldean Oracles," edited and translated by Thomas Taylor, in the notes to which Taylor argued that the Chaldean teachings, were, on important points, identical with the Platonic. He looked through other volumes and found numerous essays by Taylor dealing with the Neoplatonists. This was his introduction to Platonism and it left an impression which dominated his thought through life.

At about the same time he came across a hostile review of Emerson's works (the two volume edition of 1869) in the *Catholic World* and during the month of June read Emerson for the first time. Emerson's eulogy of the *Trismegisti* in the essay "Intellect" greatly impressed him and stimulated him to seek further knowledge of Hellenistic thought. His next inspiration was the purchase of a copy of the *Journal of Speculative Philosophy* for April, 1869, when he passed through St. Louis on the way to South Bend, in August; this contained a translation by Thomas Davidson of Porphyry's *Sentences*. In December, he procured the

[2] Quoted in Kansas City *Star*, March 3, 1919.
[3] For a brief account by Johnson of his only early acquaintance with philosophy, refer to the Introduction to his translation of Proclus, *Metaphysical Elements*, (Osceola, Republic Press, 1909), pp. xiii–xvi.

original text of Plotinus edited by Adolph Kirchhoff and shortly thereafter, Ficinus' Latin version and Thomas Taylor's incomplete English translation. By 1872, he had read Proclus' *Metaphysical Elements* in the Greek and portions of Plato in both Greek and English. In May, 1871, he started a notebook, and according to this, his own record, he quickly became acquainted not only with Porphyry, Proclus, Plotinus, Plato, and Taylor but also with Iamblichus, Ficinus, Pletho, Eunapius, Damascius, Syrianus, Longinus, Philo Judaeus, Pico of Mirandola, Reuchlin, More, and Cudworth.

Johnson was completely taken by Platonism from the beginning. He referred early in his notebook to Plato as "the greatest philosopher that ever lived," to Plotinus as "one of the most profound philosophers that ever lived," to Porphyry as "one of the most erudite and accomplished men of his age," to Ficinus as "one of the great restorers of the Platonic philosophy," and to Taylor as "one of the profoundest philosophers of the age." This early estimate would have been altered in his mature years only to include Proclus as one of the truly great philosophers. He regarded Plato as the source of all philosophic wisdom, but Plato, in order to be understood, had to be viewed through his Neoplatonic interpreters. He said in his notebook: "I lay it down as an axiom that Plato cannot be read or studied, comprehendingly, without the aid of Proclus, Plotinus, and the other Neoplatonic philosophers." [4]

The task of mastering the Platonic canon and Platonic interpreters was not an easy one. Despite his facility in Greek and Latin, Johnson soon concluded that more than the tools of philology were required to understand Platonism. Taylor's notes and the interpretations of Plotinus and

[4] p. 14.

Proclus were his early and constant guides leading back to and providing understanding of Plato, the font of the movement. Constant diligence in mastering sources and the insight of interpreters in the Platonic succession increasingly gave him confidence in his own appreciation of the essential content of the tradition. A lifetime of devotion to these materials led him to say, in 1909: "The Platonic are the only writings to which I can return, in health or in sickness, without satiety, fatigue or dissatisfaction. It matters not how often I open these golden books, I find thoughts and ideas which lift me above the sordid and material cares of life, and which are a perennial consolation and a refuge." [5]

During Johnson's lifetime, philosophy came more and more to be an institutionalized affair. Johnson was much younger than Harris, Alcott, Jones, and even Emery. The difference in age between Johnson and these other men was sufficient to mark the difference between the period when philosophy was conceived of as an intellectual substitute for religion (or defense of it) and when it was conceived of as an academic discipline. Johnson lived in both periods, longing to be essentially of the latter but forced by exigencies of isolation and training to be more characteristic of the former. His amateur standing and religious motivation linked him to the era which was passing, his research and bibliomania to the trend which was growing. As early as 1875 (when he was 24) he complained of his isolation and expressed a desire to be located in a more academically-minded environment. On July 26, 1875, he wrote to Alcott:

Intellectual sympathy and appreciative suggestions wonderfully animate the thinker. The contemplative individual, unless *most favorably circumstanced,* will find it nigh impossible to live ac-

[5] Introduction to his translation of Proclus, *Metaphysical Elements,* p. xvi.

cording to the right method. . . . It is somewhat discouraging to the person desiring to live according to the best to have his efforts frustrated by contact with those unable and unwilling to either appreciate or understand his ideas.[6]

In 1876, he wrote William Torrey Harris that he would like to move to St. Louis if he could find work in the city. In 1881, when Harris had been offered the presidency of the University of Texas, he wrote saying he would be happy to go to Texas if he could secure a Greek or Latin professorship. In 1890 and 1891, he applied to George Holmes Howison at the University of California for either a temporary lectureship or a permanent position; Howison suggested Stanford as a possibility and told Johnson that a man of his ability should not apply at any institution of less caliber. Nothing came of this. In 1892, Davidson recommended him for positions at Swarthmore and Chicago. In 1893, Harris and Davidson both pushed Johnson for a position at the University of Missouri to which Frank Thilly was finally appointed. Davidson tried to get him placed at Columbia in 1895, and Howison tried to locate a position for him at the University of Texas. It is understandable that none of these possibilities came to fruition. In the first place, Johnson was not widely-known, for his publications had not been distributed to educational institutions and he had never moved in the circle of academic men. Davidson wrote him on at least two occasions to encourage him to go to Concord, Glenmore, and other places where the philosophically-minded gathered. He did go to Concord in 1880 and on one other

[6] MS, A. Bronson Alcott, Letters for 1875. Twenty years later he was still of the same opinion. On May 28, 1895 he wrote to Davidson: "One of my chief reasons for seeking a collegiate position is that I am so isolated here that I am unable to come into contact with other thinkers and scholars or put to use such ability and learning as I may possess."

occasion, in addition to attending the Emerson centenary in 1903, but he refused constant invitations to lecture at Glenmore and elsewhere. He did deliver a few lectures; for example, at Salt Lake City and at Chicago in the 1890s. He also spoke before the American Philological Society in 1898, prepared a paper for the Philosophical Congress in Chicago in 1893, and read a paper before the Western Philosophical Association in 1902, but these public appearances were too late in life to be of great professional value. To his credit also is the fact that he and Frank Thilly were more responsible than anyone else for the founding of The Western Philosophical Association (which grew to be the American Philosophical Association), but this too was late in his career. A second reason why he had difficulty in securing a teaching position was his lack of graduate training. When he failed to obtain the Texas position in 1895, Howison wrote him that practically all institutions were then looking for men who had either received degrees from German institutions or had spent considerable time at the feet of German philosophers; Johnson had had no graduate training at all. Third, was his lack of teaching experience. It was his own feeling that since he had occasionally lectured with success he was qualified to teach; administrative officers apparently thought otherwise.

Johnson's unsuccessful attempt to secure an academic position is important because it explains to a considerable extent his increasing misanthropy, his pride in having his work printed locally, and his bibliomania. He was bitterly disappointed at his academic failure. He expressed this in writing to Davidson on May 14, 1892 when he said: "Places are given, not to merit, but to push and foreign degrees." On September 11, 1893, Jones wrote to console Johnson by saying that institutions were intolerant anyway, and that if he had secured a position he probably would have had difficulty in holding it. Jones wrote: "You could not retain it [a position] even if you could have reached it, and for the same reason. They would cast out Plato bruisily if he could have reached such a position, which he could not have done. Your doctrines endanger the craft." This was probably little real consolation to Johnson, but if he had known intimately the weakness of most institutional libraries at the time, he would have realized that his own library of classical sources was almost unrivaled in the entire country. An academic connection would undoubtedly have given him beneficial personal contacts and would have widened his interests, but he obviously overestimated the importance of an institutional position.

In any event, though sadly disappointed, Johnson did not lose heart. The library which he had started at the age of nineteen grew larger day by day. He had contacts with European as well as American booksellers, and every cent he could spare went for the books he was collecting. At first, he kept in his diary a list of the items ordered and their cost, but this soon became troublesome and he abandoned the practice. Folio volumes from Florence, sets from France, England, and Germany, and isolated but valuable additions from all the major centers of learning on the continent came flowing in to Osceola. By the 1890s, he possessed so many books that his home could no longer accommodate them. In 1898, he decided to build a separate structure, a four-room stone building overlooking the Osage, which he called his "book house"; this became the permanent repository for his collection. Shelves were constructed from floor to ceiling, and a fireplace and couch were added for comfort. Johnson's "book house" was more than a library; it was the center around which his whole life moved. Mrs. Johnson hardly saw him for days at a time, for he had his meals (scanty at that, since he was a fairly consistent vegetarian) brought to him while he pored over his Platonic studies, his translations, his editing, and his correspondence.

Johnson's library was the most important private library in that section of the country.[7] It contained over 8,000 volumes, many of them rare and inaccessible even in the largest university libraries. There were also a large number of bibliographical items and upwards of fifty of the leading periodicals of the time.[8]

Johnson's collection of sources was most extensive on the Platonic movement from Plato to Thomas Taylor. He had between 800 and 1,000 volumes by or about Plato in Greek, Latin, German, French and English and probably the most

[7] The bulk of the philosophical collection was given to the University of Missouri Library on September 25, 1947, by Franklin P. Johnson, a son, who, for many years, was professor of art at the University of Chicago. See *The Thomas Moore Johnson Collection* (University of Missouri, Columbia, Missouri, 1949.)

[8] Bibliographical materials included Clark's *Bibliographical Dictionary* (8 volumes, Liverpool, 1802), Struvius' *Introductio in Notitiam Rei Litterariae et Usum Bibliothecarum* (Frankfurt and Leipsig, 1754), Hoffmann's *Lexicon Bibliographicum sive Index Editionum et Interpretationum Scriptorum Graecorum* (3 volumes, Leipsig, 1832), Engelmann and Preuss' *Biblioteca Scriptorum Classicorum* (2 volumes, Leipsig, 1880) and numerous others in Greek, Latin, English, German, and French, providing indexes not only for classical works but also for private libraries, for Arabic literature, and for occult writings. Magazines (largely unbound and incomplete) included the conventional classical journals such as *Classical Philology, Classical Journal, Classical Quarterly, Classical Review, Biblioteca Philologica Classica, Journal of Hellenic Studies* and *Athenaeum;* philosophical journals such as *Mind, Philosophical Review, Journal of Philosophy,* and *Archiv fur Philosophie;* and a wide range of others varying from *Biblioteca Sacra* to the *Hindustan Review* and from *Zeitscript fur Philosophie und Philosophische Kritik* to the *Chess Player's Chronicle.*

nearly complete set of the works of Thomas Taylor available, amounting to some 80 volumes (including a few dupli-
cates and new editions). There were 48 titles on Plotinus,
29 on Porphyry, and 57 on Proclus. Of the writings of the
Cambridge Platonists, he had all of Cudworth and most of
More, Culverwel, and Cumberland.[9]

The wealth of Platonic material has been indicated. As a
complete philosophical collection, the library was spotty.
For example, there were none of Galileo's writings, none of
Hobbes' metaphysical works, and nothing of Locke except
his letters. Scientific and empirical philosophy of the modern
period was at a minimum, principally because Johnson's first
and chief interest was the rationalistic and intuitive tradition as it found expression in Platonism. Aristotle, the

[9] A few of the more valuable volumes were the following: Du Vallius
(ed.), Aristotle, *Opera* (Paris, 1654); Marsilius Ficinus, *Opera Omnia*
(Paris, 1641); *De Triplici Vita* (Paris, 1489 and 1511); *Iamblichus de
Mysteriis* (1607); *Omnia Platonis Opera* (Florence, 1492 and Basel,
1532); Pico della Mirandola; *Opera* (Argentini, 1504); Ευναπιου Βιου
φιλοσοφων ηαι Σοφιστων (Antwerp, 1568), and Thomas Gale (ed.),
Iamblichi de Mysteriis Liber and *Iamblichi Chalcidensis de Mysteriis Liber*
(both Oxford, 1678).

To indicate the thoroughness of the collection of Platonic sources, the
following titles pertaining to Synesius, one of the lesser figures in the
Neo-Platonic movement, will perhaps suffice: *Opera Omnia* (Paris,
n.d.); *Synesii Opera Omnia* (Paris, 1633); P. E. Baphides, *De Synesio
Plotinizante* (Constantinople, 1875); Reinhold Schneider: *De Vita
Synesii, Philosophi et Episcopi* (Paris, 1859); H. Druon, *Etudes sur la
vie et les oeuvres de Synesius* (Paris, 1859); J. Cardan, *Libri Somniorum
Synesiorum, Omnis Generis Insomnia Explicantes* (Basel, n.d.); N.
Terzaghi, *Sub Commento di Niceforo Gregorio al* περι Ενυπνιων *de
Sinesio* (Florence, 1904); G. Krabinger (ed.), *Synesii Cyrenaeci Ora-
tiones et Homilarum Fragmenta* (1850); J. Flach (ed.), *Synesii
Episcopi Hymni Metrici* (Tubingen, 1875); J. F. Lobstein (ed.), *Hymnus
Synesii Tertius* (1829); A. Stevenson (tr.), *The Ten Hymns of Synesius
Bishop of Cyrene* (1865); C. Thilus, *Commentarius in Synesii Hymnum
Secundum* (Halle, 1842); *Synesii Cyrenaeci Epistolae* (Paris, 1605);
F. Lapatz (tr.), *Lettres de Synésius* (Paris, 1870); I. Meyer (tr.), *On
Dreams by Synesius* (n.d.); *The True Book of the Learned Synesius, a
Greek Abbot, taken out of the Emperor's Library. Concerning the
Philosopher's Stone* (London, 1678).

Stoics, and the Epicureans all had their place, largely because Johnson was particularly devoted to classical philosophy. Although his general collection of recent books on philosophy was modest, he achieved a remarkable feat in amassing, without institutional connection or great resources, one of the best collections of classical and Platonic sources in the United States, if not the best.

Johnson soon learned what any ingenious person knows, that what you can't seek out can oftentimes be brought to your own doorstep. His failure to acquire an academic position elsewhere made him all the more desirous of bringing the academic life to Osceola. In this he did reasonably well, although not all of his efforts were equally successful. In the late 1870s he tried to interest the people of Osceola in philosophy, as Harris in St. Louis, Jones in Jacksonville, and Mrs. Denman and S. H. Emery, Jr. in Quincy all had done. He established the Philosophico-Literary Club and gathered together a group of schoolteachers and professional people who expressed interest in discussing philosophical themes. One man, Howard Carter, moved from St. Louis in order to join. Other members of the group included John Henry Martin, Mr. and Mrs. Van Beuren Wisker, E. O. Minnigh, J. S. Smith, Edith Ferguson, J. W. Gardner, Charles E. Robson, Ellen Amrine (Mrs. William E. Bell), C. J. Harrison, W. D. Thompson, A. W. Duff, Mrs. Ada H. Graham, Lelia Lewis, Mary Stephens, and Mrs. Johnson, a rather large group for a town the size of Osceola. After a few years the club was dissolved, largely because Johnson came to the conclusion that there were no philosophers in it; his own research had carried him so much further than the others could go in their limited leisure that he thought he was wasting his time. This experience convinced him that he had been correct in the opinion he had expressed to Alcott several years earlier: that the philosopher should go his own way and pay no attention to laymen who had difficulty in discovering what philosophy was all about.[10] Ultimately this air of superiority about the philosophic enterprise worked to great disadvantage, removing Johnson and philosophy from the audience they should have held.

Two means of stimulation remained: books and correspondents. Johnson's love of books has already been dealt with; his correspondents now must be briefly mentioned. In spite of his general distaste for travel, Johnson made a trip east in 1876 and established numerous friendships which he later continued by mail. He first visited Harris in St. Louis, where he was dined and wined by "a man in whom the philosophic genius largely predominated, a profound scholar and a perfect gentlemen," as he characterized Harris in his diary. He stopped in Jacksonville to visit Jones and was captivated by Jones' profundity as well as impressed by his library, which he regarded as better than Harris';[11] he thought Jones' commentaries on Plato ought to be printed and said that, if they were, they would "undoubtedly be the publication of the century." He stopped at Newark, N.J., to see Alexander Wilder and conversed with him on Platonic sources and translations. He met Davidson in Boston, and they discussed Creuzer, Plato, Plotinus, and Hegel. In Concord, he talked with Alcott about mystic literature and impressed Alcott with his knowledge of philosophy. Among other things, he had two emotional flurries on the trip, one in Jacksonville over a daughter of Elizur Wolcott,

[10] In 1881 a club for the study of the history of philosophy was formed in Osceola but this too failed.
[11] At the time Harris owned about 3,000 volumes.

and the other in Concord when he met Louisa Alcott. The permanent acquisitions of the trip were several abiding friendships and a few books he located in Philadelphia, New York, and Boston. One anecdote of the trip indicates Johnson's partiality for Platonism. On the train from New York to Boston a fellow traveler placed a copy of a tract called "How Shall I Read the Bible" on top of his Proclus on the seat. Later he wrote in his diary. "I did *not* read *that*. Proclus and a tract on the Jewish Bible together! Taken as wholes no antipathies could be farther removed from each other."

Johnson had corresponded with everyone mentioned before making the trip but personal acquaintance added a binding tie which made them his lifelong friends. Harris introduced him to the St. Louis group in 1877 as "The Platonist." Jones, a poor letter-writer, carried on a rather extensive correspondence with him for years. Alcott encouraged him in every plan of research and writing he conceived. Davidson recommended him for outstanding academic positions and continually appealed to him to speak at Glenmore. Wilder became a co-worker of his in the publication of *The Platonist*. These men were stimulants to Johnson throughout his career. Other men with whom he had occasional correspondence were Andrew D. White (whom he charged with attributing to Plato a statement which came from Philo, which error White acknowledged), G. H. Howison, Paul Shorey, Frank Thilly, G. S. Morris, Basil Gildersleeve, F. H. Sanborn, S. H. Hodgson, and A. O. Lovejoy. The opinions these men held of Johnson varied. Shorey thought Johnson more anxious to interpret the Platonic writings than to understand them; Lovejoy, on the other hand, invited Johnson to speak on Neoplatonism at the University of Missouri before he had even arrived at Columbia because, as he told Johnson, "You are, I take it, one of the few men in the country really at home in that literature." [12] However these varied personalities might judge him, the fact remains that he was moving in their intellectual circle and secured necessary stimulation from them. So important did Johnson regard his correspondence (and the use of the Greek language) that he bought a typewriter with Greek letters which he used whenever the subject of his letter was classical philosophy.

Although Johnson considered his correspondence significant, books were his chief concern. Johnson was primarily concerned for their philosophic content. Even in his twenties he was known for his Platonic scholarship. An H. S. Robinson of Maryville, Missouri, wrote to Alcott in 1876 about Platonic sources and he was referred to Johnson in Osceola. A Dr. Guffy of Kansas City wrote to England for certain information about Plato and he too was referred to Johnson. A reputation for scholarship at such a young age was exceptional, but Johnson was worthy of it because of his disciplined attention to sources. He gave a portion of his time each day to reading Greek or Latin authors in the original. When he was twenty-nine he expressed disgust that he had been reading only eight good-sized philosophical volumes a month. Needless to say, if he really digested eight volumes of the sort he was accustomed to read (and he evidently did), oftentimes in the original or Latin, he had little cause for believing he was shirking his philosophical duties.

Johnson shared some of Jones' missionary zeal for Platonism, but it sought expression in different channels. While Jones lectured and wrote on Platonic themes as the spirit

[12] Letter to Johnson, June 11, 1908.

moved him, Johnson pored over manuscripts trying to provide adequate translations in the English language. His first attempt at translation was in 1872 (when he was 21); this was a section of Plotinus denominated "Against the Agnostics" (Enneads 11.9). He wrote Harris asking if he would like to purchase it for the *Journal of Speculative Philosophy*. There is no record of Harris' answer, but it was never printed. On November 9, 1873, he sent Harris a section of Proclus' *Elements of Theology* (probably propositions CLXXXIV ff.). Evidently Harris turned this over to Davidson for comment, for Johnson's letter is in Harris' correspondence along with Davidson's judgment of the translation as "almost utterly valueless." Though Davidson's condemnation of this translation as "valueless" was hardly justified, Johnson's early translations were not of superior grade nor to be compared to his later work in *The Platonist* or to the translations which he published separately. In 1874 he proposed writing an "Autobiography of a Modern Platonist" which, as he described it to Alcott, was not to be an autobiography at all but rather an exposition of Plato as viewed by the Neoplatonists; this never came to fruition. Three months later (July 10, 1874) he wrote to Alcott saying that he proposed writing a biography of Thomas Taylor; Alcott was enthusiastic about this as was everyone else. Unfortunately, although Johnson collected material for it all his life, he never finished it.[13] In 1875 he told Alcott he wanted to write a "Lives of the Platonists"; this too was never completed. During this same year he wrote Harris that he was

[13] This must be qualified to the extent of saying that Johnson did print "The Life and Works of Thomas Taylor, the Platonist," a series of notes and analyses of Taylor's work, in *The Platonist* I (1881), 102–8, 147–54, 179–87. This is still the most complete record of Taylor's scholarship in print.

working on translations of Proclus, Plotinus, and Damascius, a considerable portion of which came out in one form or another, later. The first work which Johnson published was *Three Treatises of Plotinus*, printed at Osceola in 1880 and dedicated to Alcott. These were Enneads IV.1, IV.8 and IV.2; Thomas Taylor had previously translated the last two of these but Johnson's was the first translation of Enneads IV.1. The reception which these translations got was unfavorable. A critic in a St. Louis paper, after quoting from some of the more abstruse passages, went on to say: "The whole book is full of this kind of thing, but as there are only eighteen pages it may be borne. Still a canker of doubt remains as to whether Thomas M. Johnson would not be in better business plowing corn and gathering hickory nuts than doing mystic Greek into unintelligible English." [14] Johnson himself provided some explanation for such a criticism when he said: "Plotinus is a peculiarly difficult author to render into English. He has been justly termed one of the most obscure authors in any language. This obscurity is twofold: arising from both the brevity and complexity of his sentences, and the profundity of his conception." [15] Johnson's work suffered from a stilted style and from an attempt to be too literal. Alexander Wilder passed fair judgment on Johnson's translations when he wrote to Alcott on September 15, 1882, "Mr. Johnson will go on with the Enneads, but I do not quite like his diction. I do not like a cramped artificial style; and he seems to affect it." Johnson's style improved somewhat, although all of his translations were inclined to be stiff.

Several of the Enneads Johnson translated and published

[14] Quoted in Kansas City *Star*, March 3, 1919.
[15] *Three Treatises*, p. iv.

in *The Platonist*. These were I.1; I.2; I.3; I.6; and V.5., in addition to the republication of IV.1 and IV.8.[16] He also translated III.9 and printed it along with Iamblichus' *Exhortation to the Study of Philosophy* in 1907. He never finished the complete translation he had in mind. Rumor credits Johnson with doing much of the work on the four-volume translation of Plotinus put out by K. S. Guthrie.[17] This rumor is supported by the fact that Johnson and Guthrie were at odds at the time the translation appeared. Careful comparison, however, of Guthrie's work with the Enneads Johnson is known to have translated and also of their respective translations of Porphyry's *Life of Plotinus* discredits this. In contrast with Johnson's literal style, Guthrie's was free and colloquial. Furthermore, Johnson interpreted the One to be impersonal whereas Guthrie invariably used the personal pronoun; basic differences such as this make it appear quite improbable that Johnson did little more than go over Guthrie's translation and suggest changes. Guthrie's complaint in his foreword that he could get no assistance in the translation would lead one to believe that his strained relations with Johnson were probably due to their essential differences in interpretation and in attitude toward the whole enterprise of translation, rather than to argument over credit for the published work.

Johnson's greatest contribution to the missionary phase of the Platonic movement was his publication of *The Platonist* and the *Bibliotheca Platonica*. He thought of starting a journal as early as 1878 and on September 17 of that year wrote Alcott that the title was to be "The Philosopher." Alcott commended him for the idea but expressed

[16] *The Platonist*, IV, 267–72; I, 154–57, 171–72; I, 109–11; I, 164–67; I, 6–8, 18–20, 47; II, 156; and II, 157–60, respectively.
[17] Plotinus, *Complete Works* (Alpine, N.J., Platonist Press), 1918.

fear concerning its financial success. Harris was enthusiastic over the enterprise. In April, 1879, Alcott wrote Johnson, expressing the hope that the magazine would be available in time for the summer session in Concord; he said he believed the magazine would "fill a place in American journalism becoming more and more obvious to observers of the undercurrent of philosophic thought both here and abroad." In his answer of May 13, Johnson said he had abandoned the project. "The fates ordered and I submitted" were his words. The probability is that the "fates" referred to was poor health, for he wrote the letter from Texas, where he had gone to recuperate. By September, 1880, he was again planning to publish the magazine, for he wrote Alcott asking him to contribute an article to the first number. The name was changed to *The Platonist*, under which title it appeared as a monthly periodical in February, 1881. It was first printed in St. Louis, then in Orange, N.J., and finally, for the longest period of time, in Osceola.

The chief objective of *The Platonist* was the dissemination of Platonism. Johnson clearly stated the purpose in the first number.

In this degenerated age, when the senses are apotheosized, materialism absurdly considered philosophy, folly and ignorance popularized, and the dictum, "get money, eat, drink and be merry, for tomorrow we die," exemplified in the actions of the millions of mankind there certainly is a necessity for a journal which shall be a candid, bold, and fearless exponent of the Platonic Philosophy—a philosophy totally subversive of sensualism, materialism, folly, and ignorance. This philosophy recognizes the essential immortality and divinity of the human soul, and posits its highest happiness as an approximation to, and union with, the Absolute One. Its mission is to relieve the soul from the bonds of Matter, to lead it to the vision of true being—from images to reality,—and in short, to elevate it from a sensible to an intellectual life.[18]

The purpose was to be fulfilled by the inclusion of original articles, the translation of the writings of Platonic philosophers, the republication of out-of-print treatises, and the drafting of biographical sketches of important Platonists. The first number was circulated widely, in the hope that the magazine would be its own best advertising. Subscriptions were not easy to get, and continuance of the journal became uncertain because Johnson had defrayed the cost of the early issues himself. The first four numbers appeared regularly. Then came two triple-numbers and finally a double-number to complete the first volume. By this time, it was apparent that further publication would be difficult, and the second volume was delayed. Hiram Jones wrote Johnson in February, 1882 saying that *The Platonist* ought to continue but that it was too great a financial responsibility for any one man; he had sent out six hundred copies of the first issue himself but had found subscriptions slow in coming. On June 10, 1882, Jones promised to get twenty more subscribers if the second volume came out. Johnson suggested the subscription rate be raised from $2 to $5. Jones and Wilder, meeting in Concord during the summer, opposed the increase in rate and suggested instead that it would be far better to get sixty people to buy shares of stock at $25 each and proposed that an agent be put in the field to solicit subscriptions. Evidently Johnson was opposed to this, for the whole subject was dropped until the fall of 1883, when the American Akademe was established in Jacksonville. Jones then promised to get fifty new subscribers if the second volume came out, but even this did not

[18] *The Platonist*, I (1881) 1.

satisfy Johnson. In December, Jones suggested that *The Platonist* print the papers read at meetings of the American Akademe, for he thought that all of the members would doubtless subscribe on this basis. This idea appealed to Johnson, and the first issue of the second volume came out in January, 1884. Even this plan of support was unsuccessful, for in May Jones wrote Johnson offering $40 if he would get out the fifth number. Jones also said that *The Platonist* had failed them; he suggested that it be turned over to the American Akademe, that its name be changed to "Philosophy" in order to avoid provincialism, but that Johnson be retained as editor and director. It was Jones' opinion that this would considerably increase the number of subscribers. Johnson rejected the idea, and with the printing of the July number (7) the journal was again suspended. In September, Jones wrote and for a second time offered $40 if publication were resumed, but it was not done. After this sequence of events, Jones concluded that *The Platonist* would not serve the needs of the American Akademe and in March, 1885, the Akademe decided to start it own *Journal*. In order to preserve friendly relations, Jones wrote Johnson stating that he would still continue his support of *The Platonist* if it were to resume publication. Johnson finally completed the second volume between August and December, 1885. The third volume was not started until January, 1887, when it came out with a new format (octavo instead of the super-royal folio of the first two volumes). The magazine was finally dissolved in June, 1888, with the publication of the sixth number of the fourth volume. On the title page of the first number of the magazine Johnson provided a partial explanation for its ultimate failure when he said: "*The Platonist* relies for support solely on the philosophic few. It will not pander to the passions and prejudices of the rabble, and therefore can expect nothing from the multitude. We trust that the lovers of philosophy will generously aid in increasing the circulation of a periodical exclusively devoted to their interests."

It was indeed the few, rather than the many, who were acquainted with *The Platonist*. There were nearly as many foreign as American subscribers. The clientele was a limited one, far more so than that of the *Journal of Speculative Philosophy* despite the fact that in its own sphere its contents were quite as important. Its material had value out of all proportion to the size of its reading public. The translations of Platonic literature and certain of the other materials are important even today.

Johnson was the major contributor and made available a number of first translations into English. Numbered among these were Proclus' *Commentary on the First Alcibiades of Plato* (I, 38–9, 74–5; III, 1–15, 57–66, 113–16, 169–72); Porphyry's *Life of Plotinus* (II, 81–5, 97–101, 113–17); and Eunapius' *Lives of the Philosophers and Sophists* (III, 371–81, 416–23, 545–60, 577–94, 643–55). He also translated Proclus' *Elements of Theology* (I, 58–61, 94–100, 122–28, 187–88: II, 116–22, 135–38, 153–56, 173–76, 185–92), and other fragments from Proclus, Porphyry, Synesius, and Ficinus. As an editor he clearly determined the policy of the journal, oftentimes writing articles of his own on such subjects as "The Nature and Destiny of the Human Soul," "The Phaedrus of Plato," "The Human Soul: Can Its Existence be Demonstrated?" and "The Life and Works of Thomas Taylor, the Platonist."

Alexander Wilder, who was linked with Jones in the formation of the American Akademe, was Johnson's closest associate. Wilder contributed two important translations, one of lamblichus' *A Treatise on the Mysteries* and the other of the twelfth-century Arab philosopher Ibn-Badja's *The Proper Government of Life for the Individual,* in cooperation with Mlle. Peonie. He also contributed a glossary of important Platonic terms, as well as a number of his own articles. Hiram Jones made several contributions. Except for these names, Thomas Taylor's was the only one to appear frequently.[19] Johnson regarded Taylor as the most important figure to make Platonic sources available to English-speaking readers, as indeed he was. Taylor, however, was under fire during the last part of the nineteenth century for having been such an earnest advocate of Platonism that he had failed to be critical and precise in his translations. Johnson lamented this attitude and defended Taylor, as the following indicates.

Mr. Taylor's scholarship was of a high order, despite the opinion of certain invidious verbal critics who have raised themselves to a "ridiculous visibility" by the attempt to measure Mr. Taylor's scholastic attainments by the depth of their own ignorance. He possessed an insight into the esoteric meaning of the Greek philosophic text which has never been equalled or even approached by any "scholar" of modern times. It has been truly said that he knew more Plato if others knew more Greek. After all, true classical scholarship is the ability to apprehend and interpret the ideas of the Greek and Roman writers, not the mere power to grammatically analyze their respective languages.[20]

Johnson felt that Taylor had never received the credit he deserved for his work, and he became a champion of Taylor's cause. In addition to his short biography of Taylor he included numerous reprints from Taylor's writings in *The*

---

[19] Taylor had died in 1835.   [20] *The Platonist,* I (1881), 187.

Platonist. Among these were the "General Introduction to the Life and Writings of Plato," "Platonic Demonstration of the Immortality of the Soul," "On the Utility of the Mathematical and Metaphysical Sciences," and "The Platonic Doctrine of Ideas." There was no scholar whom Johnson admired more or upon whose judgment he preferred to depend in matters of Platonic scholarship than Taylor.

While Johnson never catered to the interests of the average magazine reader, he found it necessary to seek a larger audience after the financial tribulations of the first two volumes of *The Platonist* had culminated in the loss of the backing of the American Akademe. He did this by giving more time to the esoteric and occult. He had early joined the Theosophical Society and in 1884 was made a member of its general council. Even in one of the early volumes of *The Platonist* he had recommended *The Theosophist.* With the third volume he went much farther and interspersed articles on the oriental mysteries and the occult. In introducing the third volume he said:

The third volume of *The Platonist* is now offered to those who are desirous to become more familiar with philosophic and mystic literature. The favorable reception already accorded the work by scholars and thinkers indicates that it was wanted, and that there was no publication occupying the same field. The scope of the journal will include not only the Wisdom Religion of the archaic period, Oriental as well as Occidental philosophy, but philological investigations, translations, and interpretations of the later writers, the various utterances of gifted and enlightened individuals, and, in short, every variety of enquiry and speculation relating to the interior life. . . . The harmony of the esoteric doctrines of the various ancient faiths will be duly expounded. Platonism in its essence is Universal Philosophy.[21]

[21] *The Platonist*, III (1887) i.

The result was that the journal included a weird con-
glomeration of good classical scholarship and digressions
into the occult. Articles appeared on The Essenes, Kab-
balistic doctrine, theosophy, yoga aphorisms, Druidism, Persian cosmology, and astral perception. How successful this
attempt was to support scholarship by diluting it with something of popular vogue is not easy to say. It is suggestive,
however, that the magazine lasted only through the sixth
number of the fourth volume and that in the first number of
this last volume Johnson was already advertising the *Bibliotheca Platonica*, a journal which he conceived as fulfilling
the purpose for which *The Platonist* was originally started;
this fact indicates that Johnson was none too happy at
having sacrificed some of his scholarly objectives in order
to attract an audience, a principle to which he was fundamentally opposed, anyway.

The *Bibliotheca* was planned as a bimonthly publication.
Actually only four numbers came out, July–August and
November–December, 1889, and May–June and November–
December, 1890. This was Johnson's last attempt at editorial work, for he had spent considerable time and money
in trying to keep *The Platonist* and the *Bibliotheca Platonica* alive. The aim of the *Bibliotheca Platonica*, as stated
on the inside of the cover for each issue was:

. . . the critical and philosophic examination and interpretation of
the writing of Plato, Aristotle, and the Neoplatonists. The
literary history and characteristics of the Platonic writings,
philological researches, emendations of the text, philosophical
analyses and interpretations, discussions and book reviews—all
will receive appropriate treatment.

Short though its life was, this was a superior magazine.
In place of the interrupted translations of *The Platonist*

both articles and translations were complete. The contributors were distinguished people. Lewis Campbell sent two articles from Scotland, "On Some Recent Attempts Toward Ascertaining the Chronological Order of the Composition of Plato's Dialogues" and "On the Name of Plato." T. W. Russell of Oxford contributed "Plato and Greek Thought"; Charles Huit, "Platonism in France in the Nineteenth Century"; Hiram K. Jones, "On Ideas" and "Key to the Republic of Plato"; and Alexander Wilder, "Platonic Psychical Reflections," "Philosophic Morality," "The Later Platonists," and "A Study of the Phaedo." Johnson contributed a revised translation of Porphyry's *Life of Plotinus*, the first English translation of Damascius' *Doubts and Solutions about First Principles*, and articles on "Plato and His Writings" and "The Platonic Theory of Education."

It is natural to ask why these journals failed. The reason was not alone financial loss, or inadequate publicity, or an unappreciative public, or competition from other periodicals such as the *Journal of Speculative Philosophy*, the *Journal of the American Akademe*, and later, the *International Journal of Ethics* and *The Monist*, but all of these factors together. The remarkable thing is not that they failed, but rather that with such specialized motives they ever came into existence at all. Johnson is less to be criticized for their failure than praised for their existence, for they served a purpose which no other publication of the period approximated.

Johnson the scholar was more of a figure than Johnson the editor or Johnson the thinker. To understand him, both as scholar and thinker, it is necessary to realize that he conceived of Platonism, not as a point of view, but as a fountain of truth streaming from the earliest religions to

Plato, where it received its best expression, and from him to the Neoplatonists, whose commentaries and works gave it true meaning for any age. Platonism was, as Johnson conceived it, the essence of universal philosophy and religion. In introducing the second volume of *The Platonist* he argued that the materialism of the nineteenth century was disappearing, that men were seeking a more abiding philosophy, that the Concord School, Greenwood Lake, and the American Akademe were all expressive of this desire, and that Platonism, with its universal font of truth, was the medium through which the new certainty and security would come. This is why Johnson thought highly of L. A. Off's suggestion that a school of philosophy should be established, preferably in California, where teachers and thinkers from East and West could gather for the purpose of studying the similarities of various idealistic movements.[22] Johnson approved of the idea although he doubted that academicians would be interested. He said:

This idea will doubtless make the average "professor of philosophy" stare and gasp. To him philosophy is merely a mass of theories, evolved by various men in different countries, which have no particular value except as showing the idiosyncrasies of the human mind. He gives all mental speculations only a superficial examination—this is generally all that he *can* do— never even dreaming that genuine philosophy is *one* as truth is one, and that it is mere nonsense for anyone whose intuitive powers are not developed to attempt to apprehend philosophic facts.[23]

For Johnson, Platonism was an authoritative body of truth, Plato its prophetic genius, the Neoplatonists the high priests, and anyone who believed the essence of the

---

[22] See *The Platonist*, III (1887) 186–90.   [23] *Ibid.*, III (1887), 178–79.

canon a member of its sacred order. Platonism became, for Johnson, not just another, but the final, cult. This is evidenced in various ways but in no place better than in his short "Life of Plato," which he began in the following manner: "Into the world of sense, on the memorable 7th day of the month of Thargelion, B.C., 429, descended from the sphere of reality the wonderful soul of Plato, wisdom's high-priest, probably above all other men that have ever lived most eminent and renowned for the profundity of his intellect and his similarity to divinity."[24] The prophetic function which he assigned Plato was evidenced in the essay "Plato and His Writings." Here he argued that Plato's thought had largely dominated the western world but that there had been few Platonic "scholars" because most people were too indolent intellectually. He thought there was little hope for a generation of people which was satisfied with Spencer as a philosopher and Howells as a novelist. The only hope lay in a return to Platonism, study of its canon, and reinterpretation of it in contemporary terms. "Plato will never become antiquated: he wrote for all time: he surveyed things from the standpoint of the universal, and therefore, as time rolls on, from his ever-vital pages will be brought by fitting interpreters instruction adapted to the wants and conditions of respective generations."[25]

The function of the scholar, and also of the thinker, according to Johnson, was to take a body of recognized truth, make it available through translation and commentaries, and interpret it, for each new generation. The difficulty of this position lies in the tendency to promote, rather than to understand, as Paul Shorey pointed out to Johnson.[26] John-

[24] *Ibid.*, I (1881), 8.   [25] *Bibliotheca Platonica*, I (1889), 112.
[26] Letter, January 9, 1889.

son's reply would have been that when one understands he feels impelled to promote because he has discovered truth. Johnson gave his life to the study and dissemination of the Platonic gospel and, considering his isolation and the undeveloped state of Platonic scholarship in this country, he did a notable job.

Johnson regarded Taylor's translations of the Platonic dialogues as the best. He granted that Taylor was often inaccurate and that he used unpolished language, but he thought Taylor had the best "feel" for Platonic materials. He regarded Whewell's translation as useful but incomplete, the Bohn translation hasty and careless, Jowett's satisfactory and written in elegant language, but too colloquial and lacking in understanding of the esoteric meanings of Plato. Johnson was little concerned over the order of the dialogues. In his early work he seemed to prefer the order of Schleiermacher and Brandis (telescopic in nature), for he considered the *Phaedrus* to be the earliest dialogue. Later on, he preferred the more systematic arrangement of Taylor, in which classification the *First Alcibiades* is the introduction to the Platonic system. Proclus had taken this position also, for he had argued that the Platonic system begins with the investigation of the nature of man and that the *First Alcibiades* has the most satisfactory analysis of this problem.

Johnson held that Plato could be understood completely only through a mastery of such men as Proclus and Plotinus. Johnson's position in this regard was made clear in his attack on Paul Shorey, renowned Greek scholar at the University of Chicago, and explains why he spent so much time on the Neoplatonists. Shorey had written an article entitled "Plato and His Lessons for Today" in the *Independ-*

ent of February 1, 1906. He had, among other things, tried
to sever the link between Plato and the mysticism of his followers. He made the unorthodox statement that John Stuart
Mill was the "chief Platonist of the nineteenth century." He
also said that "the most conspicuous Platonists have always been those whom Coleridge calls the Plotinists, and
from Alexandria to Florence, and from Concord to Jacksonville and Osceola, they have made Platonism synonymous
with mysticism," arguing that Plato had been misinterpreted
as the apostle of sentimentalism and the antithesis of inductive science. Johnson attributed Shorey's interpretation
to the coupling of philological knowledge with philosophical
ignorance. After having severely challenged the right of
Mill, Landor, Macaulay, De Quincey, and Shorey to speak
authoritatively on Plato, he said:

It is my deliberate judgment—a judgment based on a study of
the Platonic text for over 30 years—that the true interpreters of
Plato are his genuine disciples,—falsely named "Neo-Platonists"
—Plotinus, Porphyry, Iamblichus, Syrianus, Proclus, Damascius,
and the other "refulgent links" of the golden chain of the
Platonic succession. In the writings of these thinkers alone may
be found the keys to the inner chambers of Platonic thought.

He further argued that Greek was their native tongue, that
they had works of Plato's immediate followers available,
that they possessed knowledge of Plato's oral teaching, and
that they strove to live according to the Platonic philosophy. He contended that these factors put them in a position
to speak authoritatively on Plato. Jones and Johnson dif-
fered on this point. Jones believed in gathering his insights
directly from Plato, while Johnson depended on the interpretations of the Neoplatonists.

This explains why Johnson's scholarly contributions were

largely limited to the Neoplatonists. His early work was published in the journals he edited. Then followed a period of eighteen years before his next series of translations appeared. Intermittent poor health was largely responsible for this; the interruption was broken when he published a translation of Iamblichus' *Exhortation to the Study of Philosophy* in 1907, its first rendering into English.[27] This, as well as his two remaining publications, was printed in Osceola. Included along with the *Exhortation* were translations of fragments from Iamblichus (part of the epistles on fate, temperance, wisdom, and truth), from Proclus (excerpts from the *Commentary on the Chaldean Oracles*), and from Plotinus (Enneads III.9) as well as John Norris' translation of Pythagoras' *Golden Verses*. The *Exhortation* (more commonly known as the *Protrepticus*) was the most important of Iamblichus' writings and probably had more ethical content than any other single Neoplatonic work. Iamblichus' defense of philosophy as a guide to intelligent living and as a means of achieving ablution was completely accepted by Johnson. With the publication of this work, Johnson changed his attitude toward the task of the translator and toward the public. In the preface he said:

It would be a severe and just reflection on this translation, if it could be truly said of it that it read like an original work. No accurate translation, by reason of its very nature, ought to resemble an original production. The reader is entitled to have the manner as well as the matter of an ancient author presented to him. In other words, a faithful translation will show not only *what* the original writer said, but *how* he said it. This translation

[27] Evidence of Johnson's continued activity during this period is in his projected "Platonic Library," a series of translations from Platonic sources which he announced in February, 1902. This finally culminated in the publications of 1907–09.

is not intended for the Greek scholar, who will read the writings of Iamblichus in the original, if at all—but it was made and is printed for the benefit of those who, ignorant of Greek, ardently desire to acquire a knowledge of Platonic thought.[28]

This translation was a great improvement over his previous ones, as were those which followed. In 1908 he published *Opuscula Platonica*, a collection of writings and translations. It included an address entitled "The Three Fundamental Ideas of the Human Mind," a new translation of a "Platonic Demonstration of the Immortality of the Soul" (a lengthy portion of Hermeias' *Commentary on the Phaedrus*), a reprint of Thomas Taylor's "Dissertation on the Platonic Doctrine of Ideas," and Taylor's translation of Boethius' "Epitome of the Platonic Theory of Reminiscence" (a brief section from the *Consolation of Philosophy*). In 1909, Johnson published his translation of Proclus' *Metaphysical Elements*, probably the most important single contribution he made. This was a revision of the translation which had appeared serially in *The Platonist* over twenty years previously, under the title *Elements of Theology*, and it was much superior to the earlier one. Proclus, as is well-known, was the most systematic of the Neoplatonists, and he particularly appealed to Johnson for this reason. Keeping in mind Johnson's conception of Platonism as a formal system, it seems perfectly natural that he should show partiality toward Proclus, the last, and by some standards the most scholarly and canonical, of the great successors in Plato's school.

Little time need be spent on Johnson as a thinker, for his ideas were not original, nor did he wish them to be so con-

[28] P. ii.

sidered. Johnson's principal objective was to make available the writings of those whose philosophical doctrines he believed to be true. He was therefore a defender of doctrines already established rather than a creator of new ones. Articles he wrote other than as introductions to translations were few, and none of them demonstrated any real originality. One, entitled "The Platonic Theory of Education," was read before the Southwest Missouri Teachers' Association, December 27, 1889, and later printed in the *Bibliotheca Platonica*, I, 135–42. This was merely an attempt to outline the theory of education as Plato conceived it in the *Republic*, education as intellectual discipline rather than as utilitarian. Another essay, "Plato's Basic Concepts," was read at a meeting of the Western Philosophical Association, January 1, 1902, and later printed in pamphlet form. In this Johnson argued that the distinction between knowledge and opinion, and the doctrines of man as a spiritual being, salvation by intellectual purification, reminiscence, and essences were basic to the Platonic system. These articles were typical. Whatever reputation Johnson had was due to his ardent advocacy of an old cause, not to the espousal of a new one. His whole life was given over to a study of Platonic sources and to their dissemination. He was so bound up with the Platonic "greats" that he named his three sons after them, Waldo Plato, Ralph Proclus, and Franklin Plotinus. He was forever projecting new schemes for making Platonism more widely known, schemes which ranged from writing a textbook edition of Plato to running correspondence courses. If Johnson had had his way in Osceola, or elsewhere, it is not too fantastic to imagine the establishment of a miniature Platonic state with a Platonic educational system and a Platonic academy made to order; his devotion to the Platonic causes was such that "The Sage of the Osage" would have gone to almost any extreme to establish that pattern of existence, even in miniature, which he felt was the only antidote to the materialism of the "human earth-worms" of his own generation.

CHAPTER VI

THE DECLINE OF SPIRIT

Johnson, more than any other Platonist under consideration, was a fundamentalist. Platonism to him was more than a philosophical movement; it was *the* historic font of truth. Because of this, Johnson thought it desirable to give Platonism permanent institutional character. When the foundation of a school on the Pacific coast for the study of Platonism and its reflected images in oriental religion and philosophy was suggested, Johnson quickly endorsed the project and referred to it as "one of the *necessities* of the age." [1] When it had been announced that the site of Plato's Academy in Athens had been discovered, Johnson advocated its restoration. He said:

Proper measures should be taken at once to organize an association having for its object the purchase, preservation and restoration of the place where Plato lived and taught, and where his disciples continued his sublime and enlightened work for centuries. It should be rescued from the hands of the profane, and set aside for the perpetual use and benefit of all true followers of divine philosophy. There is no good reason why, in due time, the Platonic school should not again flourish on its original site,

[1] *The Platonist*, III (1887), 278.

and again become, as it once was, the nursery of science and wisdom for the whole world.[2]

Needless to say, such a hope never came to realization. Johnson did, however, succeed in establishing a yearly cele-bration in Plato's honor on November 7, the purported date of Plato's birth. This was planned as a feast day, expressive of Johnson's yearning to provide all of the rites and rituals characteristic of an institutionalized movement. The idea first occurred to him when he was browsing in a bookstore in New York in 1876 and came across a reference to the Florentine celebration held in Ficinus' day. Later, he ran a description of this celebration in *The Platonist*.[3] It was not until 1888, however, that the first such feast was held in this country, and that, in Osceola. It was followed by one in Bloomington, Illinois, in 1889, and one in Jacksonville, in 1890. Whether or not the anniversary was celebrated after 1890 is unknown, although an invitation to meet at Spring field in 1891 was issued at the Jacksonville commemoration.

The program at these rites was of high quality, consisting largely of papers later printed in the *Bibliotheca Platonica*. For the 1890 meeting, Louis Block composed a poem to Plato, the last stanza of which indicates something of the reverential spirit in which these people met.

> Honored be thy great name,
> Holy and free from blame,
> Thou who hast shone a star unto us all;
> Monarch and wise thou art,
> Around whose placid brow
> The laurelled praises of the ages fall.[4]

---

[2] *Bibliotheca Platonica*, I (1889), 160.   [3] I (1881), 158.
[4] *Bibliotheca Platonica*, I (1890), 305. The complete poem is printed on pp. 302–5.

These natal celebrations were the climax of the Platonic movement in the Midwest, at least in terms of enthusiasm, for after 1890 the power and influence of the movement declined. The *Platonist* had already succumbed, the *Bibliotheca Platonica* never appeared after 1890, the *Journal of the American Akademe* ceased publication in June, 1892, and the last issue of their philosophical cousin, the *Journal of Speculative Philosophy*, came out in 1893. The American Akademe ceased operations along with its *Journal*, and the only one of the various Platonic clubs to continue meeting was the Plato Club of Jacksonville, which met at least until 1897. The only other similar organization still in existence by the latter part of the decade was Davidson's Glenmore School, but it was not devoted specifically to Platonic themes.

Here was a movement which stirred people in the Midwest (and the East) for a period of some thirty years, starting under mentors who were then in the prime of life and ending when these same leaders were busily occupied with other responsibilities or in their declining years. Emerson and Alcott, keen supporters of the movement, had already passed from the scene, in 1882 and in 1888 respectively. Harris had become United States Commissioner of Education and was busily occupied with other responsibilities. Jones had increasingly poor health, the death of his wife in 1891 made him disconsolate, and the taking over of his brother's medical practice in addition to his own made him extremely busy. Mrs. Denman had died in the same year as Emerson. Emery had taken up business again in Quincy, and this was such a preoccupation that he could write in 1898, ". . . I have forgotten pretty much all the technical philosophy I ever knew . . ." [5] These major figures in the movement had been

[5] Letter to W. T. Harris, February 25.

removed and Johnson, being younger than the rest, was left practically alone to provide whatever leadership was needed, or wanted. Since Johnson was ineffectual and not disposed to try to provide the kind of leadership needed, the movement gradually went the way of other historic attempts to recover the past and make it serve the present.

The leaders were strong of character and very influential. The effect upon the Concord School in 1883, with Jones gone and Alcott sick, is a good example of how important they really were. At the close of the session that year, consideration was given even to abandoning the school in view of the loss of these men. Sanborn was quoted as saying generously but mournfully that "without Mr. Alcott and Dr. Jones the school had prospered, but the 'quickening influences' had gone." [6] It is significant also that while Jones traveled to Europe the Plato Club disbanded. The leadership of Jones and others was tragically missed, once they were gone.

Alexander Wilder said in 1903 that one of the real reasons for the dissolution of the Platonic organization was the advanced age of the members. [7] One of the great mistakes of the leaders of this philosophic crusade was in making no attempt to interest a younger generation. The movement touched but one age group, inspired no allegiance to its cause on the part of younger people, and hence had no great dynamic once its founders and interpreters had spent their energies. Whether or not even this would have assured its continuance is doubtful, for forces at work upon the leaven of society were such that other and more powerful interests soon assumed dominance.

[6] Quoted in newspaper clipping (probably from Boston *Herald*) in Mrs. Jones' scrapbook.
[7] Letter to Clara Calvert, June 17.

One of the newer interests, which superseded philosophic study even among the membership of the groups concerned, was literature. This had been a prominent secondary interest with the Hegelian group in St. Louis from the start. Snider was particularly influential in its increasing importance, founding literary schools and circles all over the Midwest. The American Akademe gave considerable attention to Dante, Goethe, Shakespeare, and Browning in its later years, and Friends in Council in Quincy and the Concord School (after 1883) did the same. Louis Block helped establish groups in Chicago and Milwaukee. Lectures on literary themes became a common pastime. Monday and Tuesday literary clubs, and the like, were formed everywhere, in city and village alike, for this was a kind of culture which the dilettante could enjoy, since it evaded the prolonged thought-process involved in philosophic discussion. These groups soon roused interest in the formation of state organizations, and in 1889 a national organization, the General Federation of Women's Clubs, was established. As time went on, discussion changed from literary to social themes, inspired by a growing interest on the part of women in the affairs of the world and by the belief that these were important for women as well as for men.

American society rapidly became industrialized in the latter part of the nineteenth century. No one was more candid in his realization of the change which was taking place than Alexander Wilder, who said, "We are in new times, and we are not of them." [8] Labor problems assumed new proportions, evidenced by the effective strike in the shops of the Missouri Pacific Railroad in Sedalia in 1885. Cities experienced mushrooming growth, the population of New York

⁸ *Ibid.*

increasing around 40 percent in the period from 1870 to 1890, Philadelphia about the same, and Chicago over 300 percent. The poor crowded into tenements. City bosses became a new phenomenon in American life. Control of city utilities developed into a seething public issue. Numerous other problems occasioned by rapid industrialization aroused the social conscience. Jacob Riis published his *How the Other Half Lives* in 1890, based upon journalistic observations of the Lower East Side of New York, and many took an active interest in the welfare of the underdog. Social settlements sprang up. The New York College Settlement and Hull House in Chicago were both founded in 1889, and by the end of the century more than a hundred similar, but less renowned, organizations were active in the same field.

The new interest in social amelioration was supported by influential Protestants, and the "social gospel" came into existence. In Boston, a group of clergymen banded themselves together as Christian Socialists and adopted a declaration of faith, extremely to the "left," for the times. Walter Rauschenbusch, at Rochester Theological Seminary, argued for social action rather than pious enunciation of principles, and a chair of social economics was established at the Chicago Theological Seminary. Washington Gladden and other ministers decried social maladjustment. While not immediately effective, this movement had great influence upon the younger generation and awakened its interest in immediate social improvement, as opposed to deliberate philosophical analysis. While Hiram K. Jones might argue that metaphysical certainty was the foundation for ethical action, the needs of the day appeared so pressing as to make of his case a feeble cry in the wilderness of social turmoil.

This was a day when moneymaking was easy, at least for

many. Increasingly, men were concerned with the results which initiative, energy, and hard work, mixed with some good fortune, could achieve. They were less interested in philosophic orientation, more interested in business and social success. The problems of day-to-day existence were sufficiently varied to leave little time for contemplation of the eternal verities. Potential luxury impelled even the more sedate and reflective to try their hand at business or industry; Emery's successful venture in the 1890s was a good example of this.

The pace of life was immeasurably increased. When there was time for leisure, men wanted a less studious type than philosophical clubs could offer. They wanted escape from problems, not a substitution of one kind for another. The result was a tremendous increase in sports. This was a type of outlet that offered pleasure with no prolonged intellectual effort. Racing became a common spectator sport, with the founding of the American Jockey Club in 1866. Interest in prize-fighting increased tremendously; it was in 1889 that a diamond belt, which came to be the symbol for the world's heavyweight championship, was offered by the editor of the *Police Gazette* to the winner of a bout between John L. Sullivan and Jack Kilrain. Baseball was well on its way with the formation of the National League in 1876, and under the patronage of Albert G. Spaulding and others it rose to become the chief American sport. Athletic clubs sprang up everywhere, soon to be succeeded by country clubs when golf was seriously introduced in this country. Croquet, bicycling, and tennis all had their fair share of devotees. It was not long until America came to be known as the most sports-loving nation in the world. This type of outlet consumed time and energy which, under other circumstances, might have been devoted to study of Platonic sources.

Sports were not alone in offering easy diversion. A new and prosperous type of enterprise came into being with the development of vaudeville shows, nickel and dime museums, the cheap theater, and other forms of public entertainment. Large sums of money were spent by entrepeneurs in a wild contest to provide the newest and most unique form of sensation for the public. P. T. Barnum's circus was started in 1871 and increased in prestige and popularity as time went on. "Buffalo Bill" Cody established a "wild west show" which traveled from coast to coast, startling and amusing the public with its vivid picture of western life. While many of these activities had their greatest vogue among the new industrial class, they were patronized by men and women of all classes who were either out for a thrill or merely desirous of spending an evening being entertained. These new forms of diversion helped determine a more or less permanent mold for the leisure-time habits of Americans.

The literary tastes of the average person in the "gay nineties" were dominated by epics of American life and imaginative literature colored by the social scene. Whitman presented a hopeful picture of the march of American democracy at the same time that he expressed qualms concerning some of its aspects. Writers like Mark Twain and W. D. Howells provided satirical and critical pictures of American culture, particularly of the new plutocracy. The novel increased in popularity by leaps and bounds, with authors such as Edward Eggleston, Bret Harte, and Helen Hunt Jackson producing best sellers which were read long into the present century. Godey's *Lady's Book* and the *Ladies'*

Home Journal captured the fancy of women, and the exploits of Buffalo Bill and Diamond Dick were equally attractive to men. The reading habits of the people were expressive of an interest in the lively, the contemporaneous, the exciting, and the melodramatic. No wonder that Platonists such as Wilder could say, "We are in new times, and we are not of them."

True it was that the women's clubs kept alive some interest in the "literary greats," but on the whole they provided a superficial aura of culture rather than deep and understanding appreciation. They, again, were an example of the tendency toward spectator activities and away from individual participation. More and more these clubs brought lecturers in from the outside, many of them sponsoring a public lecture series in which they could make use of the numerous lyceum and Chautauqua programs available.

Insofar as the Platonic movement can be said to have served the needs of adult education, and certainly it did so to some extent, this particular function came to be more effectively discharged by three other institutions, the public lecture, the summer school, and the correspondence course. The public lecture was not a new idea. The first lyceum had been established in 1826. Although temporarily set back by the Civil War, the lyceum movement was a powerful medium in providing education and popular entertainment for the masses who lacked formal training. By the 1890s, the lyceum had practically gone out of existence but a much stronger movement, Chautauqua, had taken its place, providing not only public lectures but a summer school, home study courses, and correspondence work.

The first Chautauqua was founded in 1874, on the shores of Lake Chautauqua in southwestern New York, as a "re-

fresher course" for Sunday-school teachers. In 1888 the
Chautauqua Literary and Scientific Circle was founded, with
the objective of offering the "college outlook" to mature
people wishing to study at home. The program extended
over four years. In the first year over 7,000 readers were
enrolled, and in a few years upwards of 100,000 people
were following the course of study. By 1891, there were 200
circles spread all over the country, offering people in cities,
towns, and hamlets materials of a broadening nature which
they could get in no other way. William Rainey Harper,
later president of the University of Chicago, took over the
development of a summer school in 1883 and succeeded, during his fourteen years of service, in building an extensive
educational program. Under his direction, correspondence
work was carried on in college subjects for a number of
years until the resources of other institutions were turned
in this direction. The original Chautauqua was quickly followed by the establishment of smaller Chautauquas everywhere. By 1891, over sixty, with carefully planned educational offerings were in existence, though only four (those
at Winona Lake, Indiana; Bay View, Michigan; Lakeside,
Ohio; and Boulder, Colorado) now remain. Millions of people attended these summer programs and secured something
of a liberal education in this way.

The summer program offered by the Chautauquas largely
served the needs of those who wanted further education but
who had no professional interests at stake. During the same
period, the whole summer school movement made great
strides. Some of these schools were professional ones, some
were for the training of teachers, and some were offering a
year round curriculum in liberal arts. Forty-two summer
schools were in existence by 1890; by 1895, fifty more had

been added, immeasurably increasing the facilities for educational advancement, either on a vocational, professional, or cultural level. Some of these schools were expensive, but others (particularly the state institutions) offered courses at relatively low cost. Some of them provided work only for those in residence, while a few provided correspondence courses, also.

In order to spread the benefits of learning still more broadly, circuit Chautauquas were provided, bringing to local platforms renowned speakers, first-rate musicians, and other artists. By 1900 these circuits were a common phenomenon, their big tents being pitched in vacant lots for periods of a week or more in every town of reasonable size in the country.

As far as the younger generation was concerned, education was made accessible on a much wider scale through the establishment of public institutions of higher learning, particularly in the Midwest. Never before in history had the benefits of research and scholarship been made so widely available to the people of any country. The result of this colossal development of popular and institutionalized education was to make less necessary (and less attractive by comparison) the type of self-education which the Platonic groups had been seeking. No longer need people raise themselves intellectually by their own bootstraps, for education was available to them in a variety of forms. They could acquire it by attending a summer school or they could start the process by merely addressing an envelope to an institution offering work by correspondence. Platonism could not be made available so easily, and the desire for self-development which led many to seek comradeship in the Plato Club or in the American Akademe could be satisfied through other, and somewhat more accessible, means. To understand why Platonism itself (as distinguished from the organizations which furthered it) lost hold, we must remember the tendencies of the day and the effect which they had upon philosophy.

This was a period in which business and industry were developing rapidly. As mentioned earlier,[9] Platonism was in part an outgrowth of a desire to find some permanent mooring amidst the shifting tides of economic and social life. The concentration upon practical concerns, however, was too strong and too pervasive in the long run for Platonism to counteract. What was needed was not an antidote for the trend of the times, but rather a philosophy which caught its essential spirit and ably expressed it.

Science made industry possible, but it also offered immeasurable opportunities for the betterment of human life. In the last half of the century, Pasteur's work in bacteriology, Lister's discovery of antiseptics, and Crookes' and Roentgen's invention of the X-ray had tremendous practical value in the field of human health. Invention after invention led to some new convenience in human living. Sholes' typewriter, Westinghouse's railway airbrake, Swift's refrigerator car, Bell's telephone, Edison's electric railway, Ford's motor car were but a few of the important contributions of the period. Technology advanced, and experimentation became a hobby in the home and barn as well as in the laboratory. Science was a new tool with limitless possibilities, and he who chose to disregard it marked himself as one who failed to understand the world in which he lived.

Practical science was backed up by theoretical science, which sought to discover the laws governing physical nature.

[9] Refer to pp. 19 ff.

Outstanding men, such as James D. Dana in geology, Simon Newcomb in astronomy, and J. Willard Gibbs in physics, led the way. With each new discovery, men became more convinced than ever that science was the principle means for understanding the world. The universe appeared to be ruled by immutable law, best described by the methodology pursued by the scientist. This came to be regarded as true in the biological and social worlds as well as in the study of physical nature, and the work of Darwin and Spencer seemed characteristic, if not conclusive.

No one seeking philosophic understanding, in the last part of the nineteenth century, could ignore the work and thought of Darwin and Spencer. Spencer, in particular, was read more widely in the United States than anywhere else in the world. E. L. Youmans, editor of the *Popular Science Monthly* gave widespread publicity to Spencer's ideas as did John Fiske, historian, lecturer, and philosopher. Fiske became Spencer's philosophic voice in America and, through lecturing and writing, he did much to hasten the widespread acceptance of the evolutionary point of view, including its concept of progress which seemed indigenous to the American mind. Evolution as biological doctrine and as a law in nature and society was not readily accepted, however. Fiske was the target of many a critic who thought this involved the destruction of accepted religion; it did, in fact, make untenable some of its time-honored concepts. But Fiske as well as others effected a reconciliation between science and religion, so that by the end of the century their cause was victorious.

One of the great difficulties which the Platonic movement encountered was in not being alert to these new tendencies. True it was, the Platonists were not allied with the die-hard theologians, but they were sufficiently suspicious of the newer ideas to detract from the influence which otherwise they might have been able to exert. Their chief embarrassment was not so much in being wrong as in being irrelevant. This came out clearly at the Concord School when its members were accused of a bias against modern science and evolution. Harriette R. Shattuck tried to answer the charge in the *Boston Transcript* but her reply was more of a defense than a vindication. She quoted Jones as saying: "The common impression that Concord philosophy is something that is suspended by the hair of its head from the clouds and that has kicked from under it all the facts of matter, is an erroneous one. No philosophy clings to facts more tenaciously than this. The only question is, what are *facts*, and what *is* science?" [10] The Platonists, and the Hegelians as well, paid little attention to scientific method and certainly showed no partiality for it. They were interested in speculation in the grand manner and did not care to engage in the kind of thought which starts with experimental evidence and builds up its hypotheses and generalizations on this groundwork. James McCosh, president of Princeton University and a Scotch philosopher who helped spread philosophic realism in this country, said of the Concord group: "The great defect of the members of the Concord school is that they assume, adopt, and apply the ideas without any previous scrutiny of them after the maieutic manner of Socrates, or observational induction of them after the method of Bacon." [11] In an age which was increasingly partial to science and all that this involved, it was a crucial mistake for any philosophy to pay inadequate attention to

[10] July 24, 1882.
[11] The Concord School of Philosophy," *Princeton Review*, n.s. IX (1881), 54.

the methodology and concepts of science which had philosophic significance. Indifference on the part of the Platonists and Hegelians to science turned many people away from philosophy. Relatively significant is the comment of an editorial writer, who, after taking the Concord School to task for its roughshod treatment of science and its tendency toward dogmatism, said, "We rejoice that in such institutions as the Massachusetts Institute of Technology we can hear the true ring of 'truth, wherever it may lead.' " [12]

Opposing tendencies even in philosophical circles made the continuance of the Platonic movement difficult. The secularism characteristic of the general public quickly spread to educational institutions, where professional philosophers were largely to be found. Two tendencies were in evidence there, one toward historical study and analysis (which made those following this course relatively immune to intellectual controversy) and the other toward the construction of a philosophy based upon scientific method and theory. Two factors in this connection are important to note. In the first place, as need for an approach to philosophy through science came to be recognized, it made more difficult the pursuit of philosophy as an avocation. As science became more technical, so, also, did the preparation of the philosopher. Philosophy became an all-consuming vocation, and the amateur philosopher was soon outdistanced in range and breadth of thought by those who were professionally trained. In the second place, when it was clear that philosophy was not in necessary opposition to science nor even neutral in regard to it, it became apparent that the only philosophy which could hold its own was that which gave adequate place to, and demonstrated real concern for, science. The Pla-

[12] Boston *Evening Transcript*, July 11, 1881.

tonism of Jones and his followers was not dead, but out-moded. Jones could, of course, say "The achievement of Philosophy is the marriage of the *speculative* and the experimental," [13] but his failure, and that of the other Platonists, was in never taking this statement seriously, and they soon lost out to those who did.

One further factor had decisive influence upon the decline of Platonic philosophy, its failure to give adequate expression to the prevailing temper of the American mind. The men involved in this movement were deeply aware of the need for an American philosophy, but their contribution lay in providing a ready-made philosophy rather than in giving expression to one which had its germination in the moving power of American civilization.[14] It was McCosh who said that America needed to declare her independence in philosophy and work out her own unique contribution based upon the Yankee genius for practical observation and invention.[15] Even Alcott perceived that the type of philosophy which the Concord School and the other groups espoused was weak on this score. Writing his reflections at the close of the 1880 session, he said: "I am aware, and freely concede, that speculative philosophy is mostly an uncultured field here with us, the few native cultivators having scarcely made their marks on American thought; and students naturally seek instruction from foreign sources, to the neglect of matters at home." [16]

No philosophy will leave a permanent impression upon the minds of a people unless it expresses their deep underlying

[13] MS, Notebooks.　　　　　[14] See above, pp. 21–22.
[15] *Realistic Philosophy: Defended in a Philosophic Series* (New York, Scribner's, 1887, first published in 1882). Introduction entitled, "What an American Philosophy Ought To Be."
[16] August 14. Quoted from Odell Shepard (ed.), *The Journals of Bronson Alcott* (Boston, Little Brown, 1928), p. 518.

attitudes. Importations are at best improvisations and they satisfy only in the absence of something more germane. By the latter part of the nineteenth century, the pragmatic philosophy of James and others was well on its way to giving America the first philosophy produced on its own soil. In the early part of the present century a realistic movement also bore fruit as expressive of the scientific spirit of the age. The potential public for Plato Clubs and *Bibliotheca Platonicas* had found these other movements in their various manifestations more satisfying intellectually and of greater moral reliance.

The decline of spirit was essentially an eclipse of mood and attitude, deeply affected by the prevailing winds of social events and doctrine. It was not symtomatic of the decay of the American mind, but instead indicative of the growing awareness of a country becoming itself and seeking means of translating its actions into a language both native and natural.

BIBLIOGRAPHY

I. WRITINGS OF HIRAM K. JONES

A. PUBLISHED WRITINGS [1]

"On the Immortality of the Soul," *Journal of Speculative Philosophy*, IX (1875), 27–33.

"Personality and Individuality—The Outward and Inward," *Journal of Speculative Philosophy*, IX (1875), 438–39.

"Philosophic Outlines—Cosmologic, Theologic, and Psychologic," *Journal of Speculative Philosophy*, XIV (1880) 399–420.

*"The Eternity of the Soul: Its Pre-Existence," *The Platonist*, I (1881), 67–68.

"The Education and Discipline of Man—The Uses of the World We Live In," *The Platonist*, I (1881), 117–22.

*"The Philosophy of Prayer and the Prayer Gauge," *Journal of Speculative Philosophy*, XVI (1882), 16–27.

*"Man: Spirit, Soul, Body," *Journal of the American Akademe*, I (1884–85), 3–15.

"Physical Evolution and the World We Live In," *Journal of the American Akademe*, II (1885–86), 2–17.

*"Philosophy and Its Place in the Higher Education," *Journal of the American Akademe*, III (1886–87), 29–45.

"The Philosophy of Conscience," *Journal of the American Akademe*, IV (1887–88), 33–52.

"Ideas," *Bibliotheca Platonica*, I (1890), 192–215.

[1] Starred items indicate articles for which manuscripts still exist in the Illinois College Library.

"Man and His Material Body," *Journal of the American Akademe,* V (1890–91), 33–53.

*"Key to the Republic of Plato," *Bibliotheca Platonica,* I (1890), 255–73.

"The Philosophy of Religious Faith," *Journal of the American Akademe,* VI (1892–93), 193–200.

B. MANUSCRIPTS [2]

"Truth: The Old and the New," "Liberty: The Old and the New," "Toleration: The Old and the New." Lectures delivered to the Sigma Pi Library Association, 1853.

"The Eternity of the Soul and Its Pre-Existence." Concord Lecture, 1879–81.

"The Immortality of the Soul and the Mortality of the Soul: Metempsychosis." Concord Lecture, 1879–81.

"Pre-Existence." Concord Lecture, 1879–81.

"The Psychic Body and the Material Body of Man." Concord Lecture, 1879–81.

"Platonic Psychology." Concord Lecture, 1880–1881.

"The Social Genesis: The Church and the State." Concord Lecture, 1881.

"The Banquet." Concord Lecture, 1882.

"The Community of Faiths and the Worships of Mankind." Concord Lecture, 1882.

"The Relation between Common Sense and Philosophy." Concord Lecture, 1882.

"The Relation between Experience and Philosophy." Concord Lecture, 1882.

"The Relation between Science and Philosophy." Concord Lecture, 1882.

"Health and Longevity," 1883.

"Typhoid Fever," 1883.

Lectures to the senior class at Illinois College, Nov. 22, 1886–March 14, 1887. There are two other incomplete sets, for 1877–78 and for 1878–79; one with lectures 1–12, the other with lectures 7–18.

Lectures at Illinois College. In 13 sections with three additional,

---

[2] These manuscripts may be found in the Illinois College Library.

discarded introductory sections. Delivered in part or completely from 1888.

"Record and Samples of the Bore for Artesian Water at the Jacksonville Water Works," 1888.

"The Phillipino War," 1890.

"Outlines of Philosophy." Six sections, probably used in 1897 at Illinois College.

"Physics and Metaphysics," "Distinction and Differentiation of Mind and Matter," "Man and His Relations with His Material Body." Lectures delivered to the Literary Union in 1897, expected to have been expanded into a five-chapter manuscript entitled "Syllabus on Metaphysics."

"The Arts and the History of Embalming," n.d.

"Asiatic Cholera—Its History, Causes, Prevention and Cure," n.d.

"The Function of the Lungs," n.d.

"Habit," n.d.

"Heredity and Environment as Factors in Human Life," n.d.

"Heredity in Crime," n.d.

"The Idea and Cause of the Downfall of Empire," n.d.

"Knowledge: The Philosophy of Knowing: The Principles of Knowing, Universal and Constitutive of the Subjective Key and Identical Source of All History," n.d.

"Myth: The Gods of the Greek Mythology, the Ideas and Principles of their Worship, Divine Providence, Free Will and Fate," n.d.

Notebooks

"Parasite Life and Parasites," n.d.

II. WRITINGS OF THOMAS M. JOHNSON[3]

A. ORIGINAL WRITINGS

"The Best Translation of Plato," *The Platonist,* I, 15–16.

"Discovery of Two Fragments of a Cyclic Poem Attributed to Proclus," *The Platonist,* II, 134–35.

[3] This list does not include editorials, short comments, and book reviews in *The Platonist.*

"The Human Soul: Can Its Existence Be Demonstrated?", *The Platonist*, II, 2–3.

"The Life and Works of Thomas Taylor the Platonist," *The Platonist*, I, 61–64.

"Life of Plato," *The Platonist*, I, 8–9, 37–38.

"The Magnetic Mysteries," *The Platonist*, II, 131–32.

"The Nature and Destiny of the Human Soul," *The Platonist*, I, 61–64.

"Notes on the Kabbalah," *The Platonist*, III, 91–101.

Opuscula Platonica, including "The Three Fundamental Ideas of the Human Mind," Hermeias' "Platonic Demonstration of the Immortality of the Soul," Thomas Taylor's "Dissention on the Platonic Doctrine of Ideas," and Boethius' "Epitome of the Platonic Theory of Reminiscence" (Osceola, 1908).

"The Phaedrus of Plato," *The Platonist*, I, 15–16.

"Plato and his Philosophy," reprinted from the Springfield *Republican*, September 2, 1906, with appendix (1906).

"Plato and his Writings," *Bibliotheca Platonica*, I, 109–18.

"The Platonic Theory of Education," *Bibliotheca Platonica*, I, 135–42.

Plato's Basic Concepts. Revision of paper read before the Western Philosophical Association, January 1, 1902.

"The Renewal of Isis," *The Platonist*, II, 45–56.

"The Taro," *The Platonist*, II, 126–28.

B. TRANSLATIONS

Damascius, *Doubts and Solutions about First Principles*, *Bibliotheca Platonica*, I, 82–99.

Eunapius, *Lives of the Philosophers and Sophists*, *The Platonist*, III, 371–81, 416–23, 545–60, 577–94, 643–55.

Ficinus, *Exhortation to the Readers and Hearers of Plotinus*, *The Platonist*, II, 134–35.

————— *Introduction to the Works of Plotinus*, *The Platonist*, II, 2–3.

Iamblichus, *Exhortation to the Study of Philosophy* (Osceola, 1907).

————— fragments (Osceola, 1907).

Plotinus, "Divine Cogitations" (Osceola, 1907).
—— *Enneads* I. 1, *The Platonist*, 267–72, 312–23. The second portion was translated by Robert Brown, Jr.
—— *Enneads* I. 2, *The Platonist*, I, 154–57, 171–72.
—— *Enneads* I. 6, *The Platonist*, I, 164–67.
—— *Enneads* IV. 1, *The Platonist*, II, 156–57.
—— *Enneads* V. 5, *The Platonist*, I, 6–8, 18–20, 47.
—— *Enneads* V. 8, *The Platonist*, II, 157–60.
—— *Three Treatises; Enneads IV. 1, IV. 8, and IV. 2* (Osceola, 1880).
Porphyry, *Auxiliaries to the Perception of Intelligible Natures, The Platonist*, IV, 24–41, 73–95. Revision of a translation by Thomas Taylor.
—— "On the Cave of the Nymphs in the Odyssey," *The Platonist*, IV, 150–65, 169–83. Revision of a translation by Thomas Taylor.
—— *Life of Plotinus and the Order of his Books, Bibliotheca Platonica*, I, 42–77.
Proclus, excerpts from *Commentary on the Chaldean Oracles* (Osceola, 1907).
—— *Commentary on the First Alcibiades of Plato, The Platonist*, I, 38–39, 74–75 (Introduction revised in III, 1–15); III, 57–66, 113–16, 169–72.
—— *Elements of Theology, The Platonist*, I, 58–61, 94–100, 122–28, 187–88; II, 116–22, 135–38, 153–56, 173–76, 185–92.
—— *Metaphysical Elements* (Osceola, 1909).
—— *On Magic, The Platonist*, I, 116–17, translated from the Latin of Ficinus.
—— *Theological Institutes, The Platonist*, IV, 210–12, 240–41.
Pythagoras, *Golden Verses* (Osceola, 1907).
Synesius, *Hymns, The Platonist*, III, 39–41, 129–31.

INDEX

Adams, Mrs. Austin, and Alcott, 14
Adams, John, 32 f.
Adams, John Quincy, 120
Adult education, 86; and the Platonic and Hegelian movements, 7 ff.; Quincy, 120; expansion of, 194 ff.
Alcott, Bronson: on intellectual climate of the Midwest, 1, 13 ff., 123 f.; and the Concord School of Philosophy, 8 ff.; and Jones, 9 f., 69 f., 77 f., 80 f.; at Plato Club, 46; on Harris, 80; criticism of, 94; and Quincy, 122 ff.; visits to Friends in Council, 129; Johnson and, 164, 167; and The Platonist, 169 f.; death, 188; on speculative philosophy, 201
Alcott, Louisa May, 10, 165
Allegory, in interpreting the dialogues, 89 ff.
American Akademe, 6 ff.; concept of, 22; founding of, 51-68, 84; members, 52-60, 64, 85, 132 f.; purpose, 54 f.; papers, 59 ff.; Glenmore Summer School (q.v.), 63; emphasis on creative thought, 67 f.; and The Platonist, 171 ff.; dissolved, 188; interest in literature, 190; see also Journal of the American Akademe
American Homeopathist, 58
American Institute of Christian Philosophy, 8
American Jockey Club, 192
American Philological Society, 159
American Philosophical Association, 159
Art, Hegelians and, 5
Asbury, Henry, Quincy historian, 121 f.
Athens, Greece, 186
"Athens of the West," 31 f.

Baldwin, Mrs. Ebenezer, 8, 140, 141 f.
Barnum, P. T., 193
Bavaria, Germany, emigrants to Quincy, 121
Beard, Charles and Mary, 23 ff.
Beecher, Catherine, 120
Beecher, Edward, 32
Being, 85, 98
Benneson, Cora A., 127, 130 f.
Berean College, 31
Berlin, Wis., 126
Bible, Johnson re, 165
Bibliotheca Platonica, 7, 58; Jones' contributions to, 87, 90; Johnson and, 169, 176 f.; competition, 177
Bjerregard, C. H. A., 58
Black, G. V., 58
Block, Louis J., 44, 53, 76; and the Chicago Philosophical Society, 8; view of Plato Club, 42n, 47 f.; and Jones, 58, 88, 147; and the Akademe, 59 f.; poem to Plato, 187; literary groups, 190
Bloomington, Ill., 14; Plato Club, 6, 48, 79; Hegelianism in, 120; Plato anniversary, 187
Blow, Susan, 5

Body: vs. soul, Jones quoted on, 95 f.; instrument of the mind, 104 f.
Boston, study of Hegel, 148 f.
Boston *Evening Traveller*, report of a Jones lecture, 49 f.
Bradley, C. F., 58, 62, 122
Brokmeyer, Henry C., Hegel enthusiast, 2 ff., 5, 146 ff.
Brooks, Van Wyck, 18
Bryan, William Jennings, 29, 36
Bryant, William H., 5
Buford, N. B., 7 f.
Bull, Anna B., 126
Bull, Mrs. C. H., 127, 140
Bull, Lizzie G., 127
Bull, Lorenzo, 132
Bull, Mrs. Lorenzo, 127, 140
Bull, Mary B., 129
Bullard, E. F., 58
Burlington, Vt., 126
Butler, Nicholas Murray, 4

Caird, Edward, 3
California, University of, 158
Calvert, Clara, 88
Cambridge, Mass., introduction of Hegel, 149
Campbell, Mrs. Helen, 58
Campbell, Lewis, 177
Campbell, William M., 58
Catholic World, review of Emerson, 155
Causation, order of, 117
Cause and effect, 75, 101 ff.
Caverno, Charles, 8, 66 f.
Chaddock School (Johnson College; Chaddock College), Quincy, Ill., 120
Channing, William Ellery, 17 f., 141
Chapin, Caroline, 140
Chapin, Mary, 140
Charmides (Plato), 43
Chautauqua, 194 ff.
Chautauqua Literary and Scientific Circle, 195
Chicago, Burlington, and Quincy Railroad, 120
Chicago Philosophical Society, 7 f.

Chicago Theological Seminary, 191
Child, Lydia M., *The Progress of Religious Ideas*, 127
Christianity, 23
"Christian Philosophy," Concord lectures, 82
Christian Science, 62, 63
Cities, growth of, 190 f.
Clapp, Rose Nelson, 127
Classical Journal, 155
Clubs, literary, 190
Cody, "Buffalo Bill," 193
Collins, William H., 132
Concord (Mass.) School of Philosophy, 7, 8 f.; opening, 10; successors, 12 f.; and Jones, 49-52, 70; refusal to move west, 51 f., 83; founding of, 79 ff.; opinions on, 80 f.; lectures, 81 ff.; Emery and, 145; loss of leadership, 189; charge of bias against modern science, 199
Consciousness, 101, 113 ff.
Correspondence courses, 194 f.
Cousin, Victor, *History of Modern Philosophy*, 130
Crime, post-Civil War, 21
Criticism, function of philosophy, 93 f.
Crocker, Sarah C., 32
Curriculum, liberal arts, 96

Damascius, *Doubts and Solutions about First Principles*, 177
Dana, James D., 198
Darwin, Charles, 198; *Origin of Species*, 25; criticism of, 93 f.
Davenport, Iowa, 14
Davidson, Thomas, 3; dramas, 4; and successors to the Concord School, 12 f.; at Plato Club, 46; and Glenmore Summer School, 63, 188; in Boston, 148; translation of Porphyry's *Sentences*, 155; and Johnson, 158 f., 165; on translation of Proclus, 167
Decatur, Ill., Plato Club, 6, 48, 79; center of Platonism, 120
Denman, Matthew B., 125

Denman, Sarah Atwater, 14, 188; and the Concord School of Philosophy, 9 f.; and Quincy Plato clubs, 43; founder of Friends in Council (*q.v.*), 125; civic leader and philanthropist in Quincy, 125 ff.; on Plato studies, 128; tribute to, 129; death, 150
Detroit *Free Press,* on Jones, 49
Dewey, John, 3, 12
Doubleday, Abner, 53
Douglas, Stephen A., 29
Drury, Mrs. B. Paxson, 53, 58
Drury, Mrs. Charles, 44
Dubuque, Iowa, 1, 14

Eads Bridge, St. Louis, 107
Education, Midwestern attitude to, 17 f.; Plato's theory, 184; availability of, and decline of self-development, 196
Eggleston, Edward, 193
Emerson, Ralph Waldo: and the Concord School of Philosophy, 8 f.; influence on the Midwest, 16; influence on Jones, 37 f., 69; and Quincy, 122 ff.; critical editorial on, 124 f.; Johnson's first reading of, 155; death, 188
Emery, Samuel H., Sr., clergyman, 122
Emery, Samuel H., Jr., 14, 70; and the Concord School, 10; Hegelian philosopher, 121 ff.; 143 ff.; friendship with Alcott, 122 ff.; and Emerson, 122 ff., 139; career, 137-48; obituary, 139; study of Plato, 140 ff.; philosophical library, 140; second analysis of *Parmenides,* 142 ff.; published writings, 145; and Brokmeyer's translation of Hegel's "Logic," 146 ff.; in Boston, 148; return to business, 188
Emery, Mrs. Samuel H., Jr., 127, 140 f.; on Friends in Council, quoted, 128 f.
Energy, cycles of, 110 f.; of God, 115

Equalitarianism, in Midwest, 17 ff.
Ethics, *see* Morality
Eunapius, *Lives of the Philosophers and Sophists,* 173
Evolution, theory of, 25-28; Plato Club and, 45; Akademe discussion, 64 ff.; organic, 109; attitude toward, in the U.S., 198
Existence, "essential" or "vital" and material, 106 f.; cycle, 109 f.

Farmington, Conn., 12 f.
Feminist movement, 125 f.
Ficinus, 156
First Alcibiades, 180
First Cause, Creative, 113
Fiske, John, 198
Form, and motion, 106 f.
Friends in Council (Quincy), 19, 123, 125 ff., 133 ff.; 190
Fruitlands, Alcott's experiment, 94
Fuller, Louise M., 53, 58, 127; early convert to Platonism, 41 ff.; and Plato Club, 42*n*, 46; on Jones and Plato, 43; Swedenborgianism, 62

Gardiner, H. N., 12
Garretson, James E., 8
General Federation of Women's Clubs, 190
Gibbs, J. Willard, 198
Gilded Age, the, 23 ff.
Gildersleeve, Basil, 165
Gladden, Washington, 191
Glenmore, N.Y., 12 f., 63, 188
God: in Platonic philosophy, 64, 92; ideas in mind of, 107 f.; laws of, and laws of man and nature, 112; and duality of the world, 112; knowledge of, 113 ff.; two major attributes, 115
Green, T. H., 12
Greenwood Lake, N.Y., 8
"Growth," poem, 76 f.
Guthrie, K. S., translation of Plotinus, 169

Hall, G. Stanley, 3
Hamilton, Sadie G., 58
Harper, William Rainey, 195

Harris, D. H., 44
Harris, William Torrey, 37, 53, 58, 70; and the Platonic movement, 2 ff.; Butler on, 4; U.S. Commissioner of Education, 5, 188; and Alcott, 16; on American thinkers, 22; summary of Spencer's philosophy, 27; on Jacksonville, 33; at Plato Club, 46; and the Akademe, 59; and the Concord School, 80; on Emery's analysis of the *Parmenides*, 142; on Hegel, 146; reputation, 152; and Johnson, 158, 164, 167; and *The Platonist*, 170
Harte, Bret, 193
Hayden, F. S., 58
Hedge, F. H., *Prose Writers of Germany*, 2
Hegel, Georg Wilhelm Friedrich, 2, 140, 141
Hegelianism, 2 ff.; in Concord School, 10 f.; in Jacksonville, 44; spread of, 119 ff.; and scientific method, 198 ff.; *see also* St. Louis Movement
Hermeias, *Commentary on the Phaedrus*, 183
Hill, B. A., 5 f.
History, theocratic interpretation of, 114 ff.
Hodgson, S. H., 165
Hosmer, Frederick L., 122
Hosmer, J. K., *Short History of German Literature*, 5
Howells, W. D., 193
Howison, George Holmes, 3, 165; attempt to aid Johnson, 158
Huit, Charles, 177
Hull House, Chicago, 191

Iamblichus, *Exhortation to the Study of Philosophy (Protrepticus)*, 169, 182; *A Treatise on the Mysteries*, 174
Ibn-Badja, *The Proper Government of Life for the Individual*, 174
Ideas and forms, 106 f.
Illinois, 6 ff., 30

Illinois College: founding of, 16; fraternities, 30; chartered, 31; medical department, 31, 132; Jones and, 36 f.; dedication of Jones Hall, 37; members of Akademe, 58; Platonic lectures, 81 ff., 85 ff., 117
Illinois Female College (or Illinois Women's College), 31, 58
Immortality, 64, 92, 106, 145
"Immortality of the Soul and Mortality of the Soul, The," lecture, 82 f.
Individuality, and personality, 83
Industrialization, effect of, 190 f.
Insight, intuitive, Jones' dependence on, 74
Intelligence, 108, 115
International Journal of Ethics, 177

Jackson, Helen Hunt, 193
Jacksonville, Ill., center of Platonism, 1 ff., 6 ff., 29-68; Sorosis (*q.v.*), 19; and Spencer, 27 f.; clubs and societies, 30 f.; institutions, 30-32; character, 33; as teaching center, 86; personal and cultural contacts with Quincy, 132 ff.; Plato anniversary, 187; *see also* Plato Club
Jacksonville Female Academy, 31, 32
Jacksonville *Journal*, 80, 132
James, William, 3, 148, 149, 202
Johnson, Franklin P., 161*n*
Johnson, Thomas M., 53, 58, 67, 70; and the Platonic movement, 7; and Emerson, 16; and Plato clubs, 46, 79; on the Akademe, 55; and Jones, 79, 88; as Platonic scholar and bibliophile, 152-84; education of, 153, 156, 159, 166; community service, 154; death, 154; on intellectual sympathy, 157 f.; concept of Platonism, 157, 177 f., 181; and academic appointments, 158 ff.; lectures, 159; correspondents, 164 ff.; on Pro-

clus and the Bible, 165; writings and translations, 167 ff., 177, 182 f.; and Plotinus, 168, 169; and *The Platonist,* 170 f., 173; on Taylor's scholarship, 174; interest in the esoteric and occult, 175 f.; on "average professor of philosophy," 178; "Plato and His Writings," 179; "Life of Plato," 179; *Opuscula Platonica,* 183; as a thinker, 183 f.; ideal of a Platonic state, 184 f.; family of, 184; restoration of Plato's Academy, 186 f.; lack of leadership, 189
Johnson, Waldo, career, 152
Johnson, William T., 153
Jones, C. G., 57
Jones, Hiram K.: and the Plato Club, 6, 42 ff.; and Concord School of Philosophy, 7 ff., 49-52, 79 ff., 199; and Alcott and Sanborn, 9 f.; and Emerson, 16, 37 f.; approach to social problems, 20 f.; influence on Jacksonville, 33 ff.; education and career, 34 ff.; and germ theory, 36; and Illinois College, 37; philosophy of, 37 f., 71, 85, 88 ff., 117 f., 191; and Platonism, 40 f., 79; and the Akademe, 52-68; on Christianity, 62 f., influences on, 69 ff.; stages in thought, 71-84; notebooks, 74 f.; motto and poem, 76 f.; opinions re, 80 f., 152; writings, 87 f., 177; teaching technique, 96 f.; interpretation of Plato's dialogues, 89-93; and Friends in Council, 128 f.; visits in Quincy, 133, 146; reading Hegel, 147 f.; and Johnson, 159 f., 164; and *The Platonist,* 171 ff.
Jones, Mrs. Hiram K., 49n, 188
Journal of the American Akademe, 7, 48, 59, 60, 172, 177; Jones' contributions to, 87; closing year, 188
Journal of Speculative Philosophy, 3 f., 27, 43, 139, 173, 177; Alcott re, 14; Jones' contributions to, 87; analysis of the *Parmenides,*

142 f.; Emery and, 145 f.; Johnson and, 155; last issue, 188

Kant Club, 2 f.
Kellogg, A. H., 58
King, Mrs. J. O., 41, 43, 134 ff.
Kirchoff, Adolph, 156
Knowledge: and truth, 77; forms of, 97 ff.; scientific, 99 ff.; philosophical, 100
Kroeger, A. E., 5 f.

Labor problems, 190
Ladies Association for Educating Females (Ladies Education Society), 30
Lawrence, Kansas, 126, 152
Laws (Plato), 39, 89, 91
Learned, J. C., 5 f.
Lecky, W. E. H., *The History of the Rise and Influence of Rationalism in Europe,* 127
Leisure, increase of, 16 f., 192
Lewis, Taylor, 38 f., 79
Lincoln-Douglas debates, 121
Lindorme, C. A., 58
Literature: Hegelians and, 5 f.; rise of interest in, 190, 193 f.; American, 193 f.
Lovejoy, A. O., 165 f.
Lucretius, Emery's analysis of, 145
Lutoslawski, W., 3
Lyceum movement, 194
Lyon, Mary, 32

McClure, Edward, 58, 138, 140 f., 148 f.
McCosh, James, 11 f., 80, 199
McElroy, W. N., 58
McFadon, Mrs. John, 127, 131, 141 f.
McFarland, J. T., 58
McMahan, Anna B., 127, 130 f.
MacMurray College, 31, 58
McVitty, Mrs. A. E., 43n, 135n
Man, 83, 97, 104; Jones' notes on, 75; cycles of energy, 110; laws of, 112; and God, analogies between, 115 f.
Marquette, Mich., 126

Massachusetts Institute of Technology, 200
Materialism, 23 ff.
Matter, 66 f., 101 ff., 112
Mechanical arts, 107
Medicine, and Platonic principle, 40 ff.
Metaphysics, 72, 94, 97, 112
Microscopic Society, 35 f.
Midwest, 1 ff., 131 f.; Alcott on mind and culture of, 13 ff., 123 f., 133 ff.
Mill, John Stuart, 142, 149, 181
Milligan, Harvey W., 58
Mind: and matter, 75, 101 ff.; independence of, 105; discipline of, 96
Missouri, University of, Johnson collection in Library, 161n
Missouri Constitutional Convention, 152
Moneymaking, ease of, 191 f.
Monism, 144
Monist, The, 177
Montgomery, E. B., 141
Moore, Harriette, 123
Morality, 95 f., 113 f.
Moral problems, 20 f.
Moral rightness, 114
Morey, A. B., 58, 66
Morgan, H. H., 46
Morris, G. S., 165
Motion, and form, 107
Munk, E., 144
Mysticism, 181

Nationalism, and union, 21 f.
Nature, 108, 109
Neoplatonists, 155 ff., 178, 180 ff.
Newcomb, Simon, 198
New England, 14 ff., 121 f.
New England: Indian Summer (Brooks), 18
New York College Settlement, 191
Nonbeing, 98, 102 f.
North American Review, 3
Norton, Charles Eliot, 3
Notre Dame, University of, 152, 154 f.

Off, L. A., suggested school of philosophy, 178
Ohio, Hegelianism in, 6n
Order, and form, 108 f.
Organism, 109 f.
Osceola, Mo., Plato Club, 79; early history, 151; center of Platonic scholarship, 152 ff.; Philosophico-Literary Club, 163 f.; Plato anniversary, 187
"Outlines of Philosophy," lectures, 87

Palmer, Alice Freeman, 130 f.
Pantheism, 144
Parmenides (Plato), 142 ff.
Pattison, J. William, 58
Paxson, Anna, 41, 44
Perception, scientific, 97 ff.
Personality, and individuality, 83
Pestalozzi system, 31
Philadelphia, Pa., Platonic lectures in, 9
Phillips Academy, 33
Philosophers, professional, vs. amateur, 200 f.
Philosophy, 2 ff., 157, 198, 200 f.; defined, 85, 92 f., 144; functions of, 92-96, 116 f.; Jones' concept of, 97 ff.; and science, 101, 199 ff.
Physical science, value of, 111 f.
Physics, 97
Pitner, T. J., 57
Plato, 2 ff., 179, 187; dialogues, Jones' allegorical interpretation of, 43, 89-92; readings by Friends in Council, 127 ff.; titles read and discussed, 134-36; translations and order of, 180; Academy site discovered, 186 f.; see also Charmides; Laws; Parmenides; Republic; Symposium; Timaeus
Plato Club (Jacksonville), formation, 6; members, 16, 44 ff.; programs and nature of, 46, 67, 89 f.; accounts of, 42n; evolution, 45; and Block, 48; and Akademe, 55, 57; closing year, 188 f.; see also Bloomington; Decatur; Osceola; Quincy

Platonism: origin and growth, 6 ff.; center of, 29-68; lectures on, 81 f.; Johnson's concept of, 177 ff.; proposed school for study of, 186; decline of, 188-202; and developments in science and technology, 197 ff.; *see also* American Akademe; Concord School of Philosophy
Platonist, The, 7, 58, 84, 188; and the Akademe, 60 f.; Jones' contributions to, 87; Johnson and, 169 ff.; importance of, 173; introduction of the esoteric and occult, 175 f.
Plotinus, 83, 156 f., 167 f.
Pneumatic mind, 97 ff., 115 f.
Popular Science Monthly, 198
Porphyry: *Sentences,* 155; *Life of Plotinus,* 169, 173, 177
Prince, David, 58, 132
Principles, first, 92
Proclus, 156 f., *Elements of Theology,* 167, 173, 183; *Commentary on the First Alcibiades of Plato,* 173; *Commentary on the Chaldean Oracles,* 182; Johnson's partiality to, 183
Protrepticus, 169, 182
Psychic mind, 97 ff.

Quincy, Ill., 120-21, center of Platonic movement, 2 ff., 6 ff.; Plato Club, 6, 43, 48, 79, 140 f.; philosophical studies and cultural life, 119-50; Historical Society, 126; and Jacksonville, 132 ff.; *see also* Friends in Council
Quincy College (St. Francis Solanus College), 120
Quincy Female Seminary, 140
Quincy *Herald,* 124 f.
Quincy *Whig,* 139

Ramsey, Ellen, 43
Rauschenbusch, Walter, 191
Realism, philosophic, 199 f.
Reality, and the soul, 83
Religion, philosophical movements and, 22 ff.; clash with evolutionary thought, 26 f.; Akademe papers on, 61 f.; and science, 93 f., 198
Republic (Plato), 43, 74, 90-92
Riis, Jacob, *How the Other Half Lives,* 191
Rochester Theological Seminary, 191
Royce, Josiah, 3
Russell, T. W., 177
Rutherford, R. K., 140 f.
Rutland, Vt., 126

St. Cloud, N.J., 12
St. Hilaire, J. Barthelemy, 58
St. Louis, Mo.: Philosophical Society, 3, 44; Communal Society, 44
St. Louis Movement (Hegelian), 1 ff., 5 ff., 56 f., 67, 119 ff., 146, 190
Sanborn, J. H., 9 f., 139, 165, 189
Science: and religion, 93 f., 198; function of, 99, 116 f.; and philosophy, 101, 197 ff.
Selby, Mary, 44
Self-education, 21, 196
Sensation, 98 ff.
Sense mind, 97
Shattuck, Harriette R., 199
Shorey, Paul, 165, 179 ff., 181 f.
Snider, Denton, J., 3 f., 58, 70; works, 4, 5; on Harris and Jones, 11; and Communal University, 42; at Plato Club, 46; advocate of Hegel, 51; influence in literary movement, 190
"Social gospel," 191
Social order, and consciousness of God, 114
Social problems, 5 f., 19 ff., 190
Social Settlements, 191
Soldan, Louis, 58
Sorosis (Jacksonville), 19, 30, 125, 132
Soul: Akademe discussion of, 64 f.; aspects of, 82 f.; in the *Republic,* 91 f.; death and, 105
Spaulding, Albert G., 192
Specialization, 95, 116

Species, Jones on differences in, 110; progress of, 111
Spencer, Herbert, 25-28, 111, 198
Sports, 192 f.
Springfield, Mass., *Republican,* 139
Stahl, Daniel, 132
Stedman, George, 2
Stevens, Mrs. Julia P., 53, 58, 79, 88
Stirling, J. H., 3, 139, 141, 143
Sturtevant, Julian M., 32, 132
Substance: material and essential, 108; spiritual, 113 f.
Sullivan, John L., 192
Summer school, development of, 194 ff.; *see also* Glenmore Summer School
Sutherland, J. R., 57 f.
Swedenborgianism, 40, 45; Akademe and, 62
Symposium (Plato), 43, 90

Tanner, E. A., 58
Taylor, Burrel B., 124 f.
Taylor, Thomas, 38, 70; "Chaldean Oracles," 155; and Johnson, 156, 167; contributions to *The Platonist,* 174 f.
Technology, developments, and decline of Platonism, 197 ff.
Terre Haute, Ind., 119 f.
Texas, University of, 158
Theology, 97
Theosophical Society, 175
Theosophist, The, 175
Thilly, Frank, 158 f., 165
Thompson, Mrs. Elizabeth, 11
Timaeus (Plato), 43, 117, 136 f.
Transcendentalism, 16, 23, 72
"Trinity," opinion re, quoted, 131 f.
Trismegisti, 155
Truth: perception and expression of, 78; codification of, 94; and knowledge, 95 f., 100

Tufts, James H., 37
Turner, J. B., 58
Twain, Mark, 193

Uncaused Cause, 112 ff.
Underground railroad, 20
Unity, social, 21 f.

Wagnalls, A. W., 53
Watters, J. H., 2
Wayside Inn (Concord, Mass.), 9
Western, The, 3, 145
Western Philosophical Association, 159, 184
White, Andrew D., 165
Whiting, Lilian, 50 f.
Whitman, Walt, 193
Wilder, Alexander, 40, 52 f., 58, 70; and the Akademe, 59, 66; and Jones, 87 f.; and Johnson, 164, 168; and *The Platonist,* 171, 173 f.; and *Bibliotheca,* 177; on age of Platonic leaders, 189; on "new times," 191, 194
Wilkinson, J. J. Garth, 40, 70
Willard, Samuel, 8, 58
Williams, Sally, 147 f.
Wing, Emily, 58
Winterburn, George, 58
Woerner, J. G., works, 5
Wolcott, Elizur, 40 f., 65 f.
Wolcott, Mrs. Elizur, 9, 42, 47, 58
Women's clubs, 19, 126, 190, 193; *see also* Friends in Council; Sorosis
Women's rights, 19, 125 f.
Woodruff, Mrs. James, 127
Wright, Elizabeth, 44

"Yale Band," and Illinois College, 32
Youmans, E. L., 198
Young Ladies' Athenaeum, 31